The Chalk Garden

A PLAY BY
Enid Bagnold

SAMUEL FRENCH, INC.
25 WEST 45TH STREET   NEW YORK 36
7623 SUNSET BOULEVARD   HOLLYWOOD 46
LONDON   TORONTO

THE CHALK GARDEN

The Author would like to call attention to the fact that a great deal of the play is written in a special cadence: it is for this reason that the stresses in the lines are particularly marked. The same reason applies to the pause-mark so often placed within the line.

By the Lord Chamberlain's wish, and in all places within his jurisdiction, the word "violated" on page 24, Act One, must be played as "ravished," though it should remain "violated" on the printed page.

DEDICATION

To HAROLD FREEDMAN—friend and agent
of thirty years through whose endless
patience all plans eventually mature—*you*
were the spring that released the Dynamo.

Gratefully,
E. B.
(Rottingdean: May 1956.)

FOREWORD

THE CHALK GARDEN owes its New York production (and therefore its outer life) to the devotion of IRENE MAYER SELZNICK.

In America "producer" is the word for the Management. In this case it is difficult to limit Mrs. Selznick's dynamic activity by a word. For two years she lived with one end—to put on this play. She flew, she cabled, she battled. She "cast." In casting she would have ransacked the Shades.

More imperious than I on my behalf she was filled towards the play with an unfaltering magnificence of loyalty.

These few lines are written with my deep thanks and affection.

ENID BAGNOLD

Rottingdean,
   May 1956.

THE CHALK GARDEN

STORY OF THE PLAY

(2 males; 7 females)

A woman applies as a governess to a household of
position in the country in England. She is interviewed by
her employer, an old, over-powering, once-beautiful ex-
hostess of London society. She is engaged (without
references) to look after the granddaughter, whose mother
has married again, and who leads her grandmother by the
nose and exploits her caprices and her leaning towards
Freudian explanations. The grandmother gardens—fever-
ishly and ignorantly—as an escape from old age. The manservant is a classless, ageless man, unhandy with life but
with a "passion for the Right." He in turn is exploited
by the grandmother and the granddaughter. Over the
premises, unseen and chained by a stroke upstairs, there
broods the evil influence and faded grandeur of the butler
who has known all the magnificence of his employer's life
in London.

The Applicant—the "governess"—has done a life-
sentence for murder and has only recently come out of
prison. This fact swells like a mushroom cloud all through
the play, and the cloud develops flames within it when
the judge who once sentenced her comes to lunch.

THE CHALK GARDEN was first presented by Irene Mayer Selznick at the Ethel Barrymore Theatre, New York City, 26th October 1955, with the following cast:

MISS MADRIGAL (First Applicant)	Siobhan McKenna
MAITLAND	Fritz Weaver
SECOND APPLICANT	Georgia Harvey
LAUREL	Betsy von Furstenberg
THIRD APPLICANT	Eva Leonard-Boyne
MRS. ST. MAUGHAM	Gladys Cooper
NURSE	Marie Paxton
OLIVIA	Marian Seldes
THE JUDGE	Percy Waram

The Play directed by
ALBERT MARRE
with Setting and Costumes by
CECIL BEATON

It was presented in London, co-inciding with the run in New York, by H. M. Tennent Ltd., at the Haymarket Theatre on 11th April 1956, with the following cast:

MISS MADRIGAL (First Applicant)	Dame Peggy Ashcroft
MAITLAND	George Rose
SECOND APPLICANT	Ruth Lodge
LAUREL	Judith Stott
THIRD APPLICANT	Phyllis Relph
MRS. ST. MAUGHAM	Dame Edith Evans
NURSE	Mavis Walker
OLIVIA	Rachel Gurney
THE JUDGE	Felix Aylmer

The Play directed by
SIR JOHN GIELGUD
with Setting by
REECE PEMBERTON

8

TIME: *The present.*

PLACE: *A room in a manor house, Sussex, England.*

ACT ONE
A day in June.

ACT TWO
Two months later.

ACT THREE
Twenty minutes later.

The Chalk Garden

ACT ONE

TIME: *The present.*

PLACE: *A room in one of those Manor Houses which border a Village Green in a village in Sussex. The soil is lime and chalk. The village is by the sea.*

From one high window in the room, preferably downstage Left, the personages on the stage can see, when standing up, the life that goes on on the Village Green.

Back stage there is a wide French window, standing open, that gives on to the garden. On stage Left is a door leading to the main part of the house. A corridor (much grander than the room seen in the Set) leads presumably to the front door, to dust-sheeted entertaining rooms, and a curving staircase leads to the rooms upstairs. Farther upstage Left is a baize door leading to MAITLAND'S pantry.

A small door opens downstage Right to show a narrow flight of stairs leading to Pinkbell's bedroom. If another door to the garden would be useful it is placed downstage Right.

Beyond the open French window a bosky, belillied garden runs slightly uphill. A June gale blows. The room has a look of vigour and culture. The furniture is partly inherited, partly bought in MRS. ST. MAUGHAM'S young days. It is probably Regency, but the owner of this house does not tie herself to anything. She has lived through many moods, and is a jackdaw for the Curious and Strange. The only object necessarily described is her work-table back stage, running the length of the windows. It is a rough table, rather high and long. Under it lie in disorder baskets, garden trugs, a saw, two long-handled grass-cutters, a tin of Abol, a sack of John Innes potting soil, a log basket full of raffia, and rubber clogs, etc. On top of the table are strewn scissors, string, garden-ing books, flower catalogues, gardening gloves, a small watering can for vases in the room, a trowel, etc.

Beneath the high window that looks out on the Village Green is a round table that can be used in Act Two as a dining table. There is also somewhere in the room another small table, or light card table, which can be used in Act Two for LAUREL and MISS MADRIGAL. It should be noted however that the furniture in the room is that of a sitting room and is merely adapted for purposes of meals. The sideboard, for instance, should really be a side table of some sort, or a commode,—an improvisation.

ON CURTAIN UP there are four chairs in a row, facing towards Stage Right. Three are empty. Over the back of the Downstage one is draped a small ragged feather boa as though it had slipped from someone's shoul-der. MISS MADRIGAL sits on the Upstage chair. She is an enigmatical, contained woman, neat and non-committal in dress—with fine eyes, and she has the still look of an eagle at rest upon a rock.

AS THE CURTAIN RISES, MAITLAND opens the front door (leaves it open) and shows in a rapid LITTLE LADY (the next applicant). She comes in quickly, like a bird over a lawn, going behind Left chairs to below them.

LITTLE LADY. *(A-flutter)* Good morning. May one sit?
(MADRIGAL *does not answer.* MAITLAND *nods and
exits up Right to garden.* LITTLE LADY *sits, leaving
a chair vacant between herself and* MISS MADRIGAL.
*She takes off her gloves, and places them with her
bag on this vacant chair. She hides her hands; it is a
trick of hers.)*
Lovely, blowy weather— Are you too here for the interview?
(The DOORBELL rings.)
As I came in I saw a lady going out. In a temper.

(THE THIRD LADY—*whose beauty is decayed—sails in
from the hall. She carries a parasol, wears a chiffon
scarf on her head.)*

MAITLAND. *(Returning up Right)* Who let you in?
THIRD LADY. The front door stood wide open—so
humane. *(Going down Left Centre. To other* TWO APPLI-
CANTS) Good morning! How do you do?
MAITLAND. Have you a letter? *(Right of chair to front
of sofa.)*
THIRD LADY. *(Facing him)* I wouldn't have come, dear,
if I hadn't had a letter. *(Waves it at him)* Are you the
butler?
MAITLAND. I am the manservant.
THIRD LADY. A world of difference! *(Letter in bag,
scarf off.)* In my days it was thought common to wear a
white coat. A relic of our occupation in India. Now over.
In those days only worn in Cheltenham. *(Turning towards
APPLICANTS.)*
MAITLAND. Will you sit down please.
THIRD LADY. *(To above table)* In those days—in the
Hill Stations, I was thought to have extra-ordinary charm!
(Turning suddenly to him) Is this a house where there
are gentlemen?
MAITLAND. *(Stiffly)* I am not to give information.
THIRD LADY. *(Puts scarf on back of chair)* But you have
only to nod. *(Fingering things on the Centre table)*

—gardening gloves— Nicotine for wood lice— Is your lady going up in the world? Or coming down? One has to be so careful.

MAITLAND. *(Outraged)* Mrs. St. Maugham has a house in Belgrave Square!

THIRD LADY. But you are left in the country, I suppose, when she goes up for the Season?

MAITLAND. *(Shortly)* Madam is past the Seasons. Take a chair, please.

THIRD LADY. Where are the entertaining rooms?

MAITLAND. They are under dust sheets.

THIRD LADY. *(Takes scarf and turns to* APPLICANTS*)* Not that I am applying for the post, you know—not really!

LITTLE LADY. *(Gasping)* Not applying?

THIRD LADY. I came— *(Behind chairs)* I came to have a peep! *(Improvising)* So nostalgic— *(On to second step.)*

MAITLAND. *(Crossing over Left)* Where are you off to?

THIRD LADY. *(Thrusting sunshade into his hand. Tying the chiffon scarf round her hair. Mockingly)* Such a wind out. So rough and rude in summer—

MAITLAND. But you're not going!

THIRD LADY. *(Teasing him. But it is the truth)* I could not *think* of staying in a house—where there is not even a nephew! *(Takes sunshade back.)*

MAITLAND. *(On to second step)* But what shall I tell *her?*

THIRD LADY. *(With ancient mischief)* —that people who advertise—are never quite of one's world! *(She goes by the front door.)*

(MAITLAND *exits to pantry.*

The girl, LAUREL, *comes down the stairs or in from garden, according to Set. She is sixteen, dressed in blue jeans, blue slippers and a white jumper. She is wearing a large diamenté necklace, a pearl bangle, and a wide sash of pink silk round her waist. She carries a long pearl necklace.)*

LAUREL. *(With insolent calm. On second step)* My grandmother had a hundred and seven answers. *(Silence. Comes down Centre)* I mean to her advertisement for someone to look after me.

LITTLE LADY. *(Rising, propitiatory, puts out a nervous hand)* You are the young lady—who requires a companion? *(Her poor, nervous hand steals out.)*

LAUREL. I never shake hands. It's so animal.

(LITTLE LADY *sinks back.)*

(Towards sofa—ties sash in a bow) So one of you has come to look after me? We were expecting four applicants —the ones my grandmother selected from the letters. *(Turns)* So now there are only two to choose from. *(Centre again. To the* LITTLE LADY) What are your qualifications?

LITTLE LADY. *(Anxious, leaning forward)* Frobel-trained. Long ago. But Frobel-trained. *(Almost in a whisper)* And patience.

LAUREL. Would you have patience with me?

LITTLE LADY. I am so fond of young people.

LAUREL. I set fire to things. I am not allowed alone, except in the garden. *(Turns away. Sits armchair.)*

LITTLE LADY. *(Carrying on bravely)* Such lovely weather for the garden. *(Rises. Crosses to above table)* The advertisement said "with handicraft." I am clever with my fingers. I am fond of making pretty things. *(Coy)* Now—can you make a lampshade?

LAUREL. All the lampshades here are made already.

LITTLE LADY. *(Confidential)* Will you tell me, dear, of what does the family consist?

LAUREL. Of my grandmother. Of me. And Maitland. *(Pointing to ceiling)* And the terrible old man upstairs. And his hospital nurse.

LITTLE LADY. *(Horrified)* Your—grandfather?

LAUREL. Mr. Pinkbell was always the butler. Now he has a stroke.

LITTLE LADY. *(Glancing to the pantry)* Who was that then?

LAUREL. That was Maitland. He wears a grocer's coat.

You get them for a guinea. Mr. Pinkbell, of course, used to wear a black one and have a footman.

LITTLE LADY. But is there no one else?

LAUREL. Oh we are rich! *(Rises. Crosses down stage to behind Left chairs)* If we have only one servant it is part of my grandmother's newest theory about life. She says true devotion is only to be got when a man is worked to death and has no rival. *(Fingers feather boa distastefully)* Maitland plays games with me so he has his hands full.

LITTLE LADY. *(To front of Left chairs)* But have you no mother?

LAUREL. *(Leans against window table)* My mother married again. She married for love.

(LITTLE LADY *sits third chair.*)

It has given me an adolescent repugnance to her. My case is practically in Freud. My grandmother will explain it to you. *(Leans against wall above window.)*

LITTLE LADY. And where is your father?

LAUREL. My father shot himself when I was twelve. I was in the room. *(Steps in behind* MADRIGAL*)* And what are *your* qualifications?

MADRIGAL. I prefer to wait for your grandmother.

LAUREL. *(Interested in this answer)* Are you Scotch?

MADRIGAL. I was born in Barbados.

LAUREL. Where do you live?

MADRIGAL. In my room.

LAUREL. How do you take to me?

MADRIGAL. You are not what I am used to.

LAUREL. I am fond of painting. Can you paint?

MADRIGAL. What I cannot do is to wait much longer.

LAUREL. *(Going to door up Centre)* Oh, she'll come! Grandloo will come! She is working in the garden. She's a great gardener, but nothing grows for her.

(A LADY *is seen at the front door. She rings the bell, and* MAITLAND *comes out to answer it.* LAUREL *has come down Right of* MADRIGAL.)

Do wait. You may be the one we are looking for.

MAITLAND. *(Comes hurrying to the chair for the*

feather boa. As he picks it up, he sees LAUREL) She says
she left this behind. *(To* LAUREL, *who runs to door up
Right)* What are you doing wearing Madam's necklaces?
(He follows her) Off with them! You've been upstairs
and I thought I'd left you happy in the garden.
    *(She takes off the necklaces and gives them to him—
    hiding the bangle behind her.)*
Out you go! I've got a bonfire laid at the top there! You
shall light it when I get a minute.

(LAUREL *puts the bangle in his hand and goes out.* MAIT-
    LAND *runs to the front door with the boa. Hands it
    back to the unseen caller.)*

    LITTLE LADY. *(To* MADRIGAL) Do you think it's all
true?
    MADRIGAL. *(Indifferently)* I should think it unlikely.

(MAITLAND *returns and puts jewels in cigar box on up
    stage table.)*

    LITTLE LADY. *(Rises. Below chairs to behind* MADRI-
GAL) For the interview—when the interview—ought we
to be together?
    MAITLAND. *(Turns, cigar box in hand)* One of you
ladies can wait in the drawing room. It's dust-sheeted, but
there's a chair. *(Puts box under Centre table, then takes
gloves and nicotine to up stage table.)*
    LITTLE LADY. One must be fair! Let it be me! This
lady—
    (As she reaches over for her handbag, MADRIGAL
    picks hers up, putting it on her lap.)*
(Tone changing after precaution) —was before me. *(She
goes into the hall. Much commoner)* When you're ready,
you just call, dear! *(She makes for the drawing room, then
turns and goes quickly out by the front door.)*

(Neither MAITLAND *nor* MADRIGAL *has been watching
    her.)*

MAITLAND. *(Turning from up stage table, looking Right)* Whew!

MADRIGAL. She's a little light-fingered.

MAITLAND. *(Looking on Centre table)* That one? Oh!

MADRIGAL. No more than a box of matches or the tatler.

MAITLAND. Do you know her?

MADRIGAL. No. But I have met those hands before. Many times.

MAITLAND. Met her hands? *(Goes into the hall)* She's gone! Out of the front door. *(Takes bowl of flowers from hall table.)*

MADRIGAL. They were none of them solid applicants.

MAITLAND. *(Behind her)* But they wrote to Madam!

MADRIGAL. It's how they spend their days. They answer advertisements.

MAITLAND. *(Puts bowl on window table. Picks up writing-pad)* Not meaning to take the job!

MADRIGAL. *(Absently)* They are always in two minds. It makes a change for them— *(At her own words she goes a bit off track)* —and then too she has a garden.

MAITLAND. It's you who have two minds, it seems! *(Eyeing her anxiously)* Don't you be flitting! *(Crossing down stage to desk)* If there's nobody here—after all the advertising—who do you think's going to get the brunt!

MADRIGAL. *(To herself)* I cannot hope to be acceptable —at the first undertaking.

MAITLAND. *(Pad on desk. Picks up four letters)* You don't need to worry! Madam's up a tree! Today's the deadline.

MADRIGAL. *(Prim and yet nervous)* There's an urgency?

MAITLAND. *(Crosses above chair to her)* Madam's mad for the child! She's got her daughter coming. A shy lady. A nice one. But there's wheels within wheels. If you ask me—Madam's afraid she'll take the child. *(Letters on table.)*

MADRIGAL. The child's outlandish!

MAITLAND. Only what *Madam* makes her. I can explain

her! Nurse and Nanny I bin to her! *(Crosses down stage to door down Right.)*

MADRIGAL. In a house like this—would I be suitable?

MAITLAND. She'll take you! Madam loves the unusual! *(Opens door)* It's a middle class failing—she says—to run away from the unusual! *(Puts things on stairs.)*

VOICE. *(From offstage Right in the garden)* Maitland! *(Coming nearer)* Maitland!

MAITLAND. Madam! *(Closes door. Up to Right end of up stage table.)*

(MRS. ST. MAUGHM *is seen coming from the garden. She is pushing a wicker garden trolley loaded with gardening tools.)*

VOICE. Maitland! *(Head through Left half of window)* Are my teeth on the table? My bottom teeth—

MAITLAND. *(Searching)* There's nothing.

VOICE. Then I must have left them in the greenhouse. *(She moves on with trolley and disappears.)*

MAITLAND. *(Going out to her)* Here! Wait, Madam— Here they are—wrapped in a handkerchief!

(MAITLAND *gives her the handkerchief and returns, followed by* MRS. ST. MAUGHAM. *She is an old, overpowering, once beautiful, ex-hostess of London society.)*

(Re-entering) There's a dentist taken the empty house by the church. He might make you comfortable!

(MADRIGAL *rises.*)

MRS. ST. MAUGHAM. *(Right of* MAITLAND. *Takes gloves off)* I've tried all the dentists! You can't fit false teeth to a woman of character. *(Gloves on up stage table. Hat off)* As one gets older and older, the appearance becomes such a bore. *(She sees* MADRIGAL*)* Good morning. *(Displeased— to* MAITLAND*)* But I expected four applicants!

MAITLAND. Four came. Three have gone.

MRS. ST. MAUGHAM. And one wrote me such a good letter! Gone?

MAITLAND. But I've kept this one.

MRS. ST. MAUGHAM. *(To* MADRIGAL*)* Shall we sit? *(Gives* MAITLAND *her hat)* You can go, Maitland.

(MADRIGAL *crosses down stage to sofa and sits.* MAITLAND *exits to pantry.)*

(With a sudden and alarming charm) Now what questions do total strangers put to one another? *(Sits armchair.)*

MADRIGAL. *(Colourlessly)* The name is Madrigal.

(MRS. ST. MAUGHAM *takes spectacles from apron pocket and selects the "Madrigal" letter from the table.)*

I am the daughter of the late Ronald Bentham Madrigal, Rajputuna Hussars, Indian Army. He was the son of General Bentham Madrigal—the Honourable East India Company.

MRS. ST. MAUGHAM. No, no! That you can't be! The Honourable East India Company was dissolved in 1860! I'm an expert! My great-grandfather was Tarr Bethune, Governor of Madras, tried for corruption in 1859 and found guilty!

MADRIGAL. *(Calmly)* My grandfather had my father at the age of seventy-five.

MRS. ST. MAUGHAM. *(Admitting the point)* That might make it possible. What experience have you?

MADRIGAL. I have small private means. I have not taken such a post before.

MRS. ST. MAUGHAM. Why do you apply to me?

MADRIGAL. The advertisement tempted me. I have been —somewhat alone.

MRS. ST. MAUGHAM. You will be able, I suppose, to give me references?

MADRIGAL. *(Coldly)* That will be difficult.

MRS. ST. MAUGHAM. What?

MADRIGAL. In fact impossible.

(The door Right opens and a hospital NURSE *in full uni-*

form comes into the room. She carries a breakfast tray.)

NURSE. *(Stiff, reproachful)* We've been ringing, Mrs. St. Maugham.

MRS. ST. MAUGHAM. I heard nothing!

NURSE. *(Taking tray, behind sofa, to up stage table. Acid)* Our breakfast tray was late again.

MRS. ST. MAUGHAM. One can't have everything!

NURSE. Mr. Pinkbell says one should have a great deal more. *(She exits, flouncing.)*

MRS. ST. MAUGHAM. One of his cross mornings. Ask *me* questions, Miss Madrigal.

MADRIGAL. Does one have a room to oneself?

(MAITLAND enters. Takes tray from up stage table.)

MRS. ST. MAUGHAM. Life without a room to oneself is a barbarity. Luncheon here with me and my granddaughter. Your evening meal served in your room on a tray—

MAITLAND. *(Stopping on way out)* That can't be done!

MRS. ST. MAUGHAM. *(Automatically)* Ma'am.

MAITLAND. *(As automatically)* Ma'am.

MRS. ST. MAUGHAM. And why can't it?

(TELEPHONE rings off Left.)

MAITLAND. *(Left of her)* Because I shall be busy serving at Madam's table.

MRS. ST. MAUGHAM. I hear the telephone.

(MAITLAND exits.)

Now—now—Miss Madrigal! We are so continuously interrupted— Are you Church of England?

MADRIGAL. *(Whose mind is only on the telephone)* My religion is private. I should tell you—in case you should ask me to—I don't answer the telephone.

MRS. ST. MAUGHAM. *(Immediately interested)* For what reason?

MADRIGAL. I prefer not to. *(As though realizing by MRS.*

Sт. Maugham's *attitude that more explanation is needed)*
It disturbs me to join two worlds.

Mrs. Sт. Maugham. Which—?

Madrigal. The outside . . . and the inside one.

Maitland. *(Returning)* They want you to open the
village Summer Festival.

Mrs. Sт. Maugham. Are they holding on?

Maitland. They are.

Mrs. Sт. Maugham. Ask them what attendance they
can insure? Last time I opened something there was nobody there.

Maitland. Madam is so unpopular.

Mrs. Sт. Maugham. How do you know?

Maitland. I hear it on all sides.

Mrs. Sт. Maugham. They tell you that when I send
you down to the post. Give me my engagement book.
(Spectacles out.)

Maitland. That's last year's.

Mrs. Sт. Maugham. Give it me all the same. The dates
are not so different. Have you lived in a village, Miss
Madrigal?

(Maitland, *now Right of her, hands her the book.)*

Madrigal. *(Mumbling)* No, Mrs. St. Maugham—

Mrs. Sт. Maugham. *(Vaguely leafs through book)* All
the graces of life here go unvalued. In a village one is down
to the bones of things. When I was at my height—though
I lived here—I never knew them! They were waiting for
my old age like wolves it seems! Tell them I won't open it.
(Hands book back.)

(Maitland *returns it to desk and exits to pantry.)*
Ah—where were we? My advertisement asks for handicraft. What handicraft do you suggest?

Madrigal. I have ornamented a chapel.

Mrs. Sт. Maugham. With your needle?

Madrigal. With my brush. I have painted a twining
plant on the altar candles.

Mrs. Sт. Maugham. *(Immediately interested)* But—

as the candles burnt down the painting must have melted away!

MADRIGAL. *That* was the beauty of *it!* Is this a quiet house?

MRS. ST. MAUGHAM. Absolutely.

(Wild SCREAMS are heard off stage up the garden.
MAITLAND *bursts in, rushes through to the garden.)*

MAITLAND. That child again— *(Disappears up Right.)*

MRS. ST. MAUGHAM. *(Calm)* My daughter's child. My granddaughter. She's so fond of screaming.

MADRIGAL. While I was waiting a young girl passed through the room.

MRS. ST. MAUGHAM. That was she! She lives with me. Did she say anything?

MADRIGAL. *(Colourless)* Nothing of consequence.

MRS. ST. MAUGHAM. Not the suicide of her father?

MADRIGAL. I think she mentioned it!

MRS. ST. MAUGHAM. *(Delighted)* Oh Laurel—to make a drama—! He died—poor man—of his liver!

MADRIGAL. *(As though it were a foible)* She does not care for the truth?

MRS. ST. MAUGHAM. No. But I encourage her. She loves a small limelight! One must be tender with her. Alas, he died when she was three. Rich and a fine estate. Four Van Dykes and unique Sheraton furniture. *(Bitterly)* Her mother's one success— *(Rises. To Left of table)* But why speak of it! She married again.

MADRIGAL. And where *is* her mother?

MRS. ST. MAUGHAM. She follows the drum—as they say—in Arabia. Stationed abroad is the term, but I dislike military language. She is coming by ship—I am expecting her.

MADRIGAL. *(Rising)* Would you sooner postpone—

MRS. ST. MAUGHAM. *(To her)* But she does not come here!—I should be your employer.

MADRIGAL. *(Cautiously)* She *is* coming?

MRS. ST. MAUGHAM. In front of the child—we don't mention it. She is coming.

(MADRIGAL *sits again.*)

One does not know why, though I shrewdly suspect it. *(Pauses, looks at miniature on the table)* I have an unworldly daughter. She was always crying out after being simple. That's hard to understand. It seems such a waste, with all the chances of life, to want to be simple. Privilege and power make selfish people—but gay ones— *(Breaks off)* Forgive me, Miss Madrigal, for being personal. *(Miniature back)* But irritation is like a rash on the heart! *(Sits again.)*

MADRIGAL. *(To change the subject)* The child—is she fond of her stepfather?

MRS. ST. MAUGHAM. *(Indifferent)* I never asked. His rank is Colonel. My grand-daughter has developed an interesting mother-hatred, which is clearly explained in Freud. You have had experience? You feel competent to deal with such things?

MADRIGAL. *(Dreamily)* For the worse—or the better—

MRS. ST. MAUGHAM. You seem absent in mind!

MADRIGAL. *(Pulling herself together again)* Not in mind—but in manner. *(Pursily)* The child is naturally alienated—that a sexlife has broken out again in her mother.

MRS. ST. MAUGHAM. You put it well. Exactly. The child was frenzied.

(The house PHONE rings.)

When nothing would stop the wedding—she ran from the hotel into the dark—

(Second RING.)

MADRIGAL. There seems to be a bell ringing.

(PHONE stop.)

MRS. ST. MAUGHAM. *(Getting up and talking as she crosses Right to house telephone)* —and by some extra-ordinary carelessness she was violated in Hyde Park at the age of twelve. It has upset her nerves. We are waiting as it were for calmer weather. *(Picking up house telephone)* You want me, Pinkbell? One moment— *(Hand over phone)* Of course we put it less strongly to her mother. Apart from certain fixations connected with fire, she is a charming intelligent girl. I should value your impressions. *(Into phone)* What's that! *(Listens)* I did. I ordered it. The Extract of Humus—for the seed boxes. *(Listening)* It should have come. I'll ring. I'll ring and ask him. *(Is about to put the receiver from her but is recalled by the VOICE)* I know! I know! But one can't get perfection, Pinkbell! *(Replaces receiver on hook. To herself)* Oh . . . isn't jealousy terrible! *(Moving above chair.)*

MADRIGAL. *(With surprising force)* Yes.

MRS. ST. MAUGHAM. You made me jump. He's my butler. Forty years my butler. Now he's had a stroke but he keeps his finger on things. *(Rings handbell. Keeps bell.)*

MADRIGAL. He carries on at death's door.

MRS. ST. MAUGHAM. His standards rule this house.

MADRIGAL. *(Absently)* You must be fond of him.

MRS. ST. MAUGHAM. Alas no. *(Below chair)* He trains Maitland—but now Maitland won't go near him. But I shall overcome it. *(Sits.)* He's so good with the garden. *(Rings bell again, over back of chair.)*

MADRIGAL. Maitland?

MRS. ST. MAUGHAM. Pinkbell. He directs mine from his window. All butlers dream of gardening. *(Puts bell on table)* We spoke of references. Who will speak for you?

MADRIGAL. *(In her sing-song voice)* No one will speak for me— Extract of Humus is too rich for summer bienials.

(MAITLAND *enters up Centre from garden. To Left of* MRS. ST. MAUGHAM.)

MRS. ST. MAUGHAM. Has a bag of humus been delivered at the back door?

MAITLAND. There's a sack there.

MRS. ST. MAUGHAM. When did it come?

MAITLAND. Days ago.

MRS. ST. MAUGHAM. And you walk by it and ignore it! How do you know someone hasn't sent me a brace of pheasants! Mr. Pinkbell says you must report and at once everything that comes to the back door.

MAITLAND. *(Suddenly, reaching his limit) I won't take orders from the old bastard!*

MRS. ST. MAUGHAM. Am I to have trouble with you, Maitland?

MAITLAND. *(Breaking)* Oh, if I could please and be sure of myself!

MRS. ST. MAUGHAM. *(Quiet, menacing)* Maitland—

MAITLAND. Oh, if things would go smoothly!

MRS. ST. MAUGHAM. *Maitland! (With deliberation and distinctness)* Bring me the Crême de Menthe and two glasses.

(MAITLAND's *chest fills with emotion. He seems about to burst. He obeys and rushes out through his door.)* *(Fanning her face with hankerchief)* Touch and go! How frail is authority. What were you saying?

MADRIGAL. When?

MRS. ST. MAUGHAM. About humus and summer biennials.

MADRIGAL. *(Tonelessly, sleepwalkingly)* Don't pep up the soil before birth. It leads them on to expect—what life won't give them.

MRS. ST. MAUGHAM. *(Leaning forward)* Speak louder!

MADRIGAL. *(With awkward and unstable loudness)* What life won't give them.

MRS. ST. MAUGHAM. *(Suddenly reminded)* What was that plant you painted on the candles?

MADRIGAL. *(With inner pleasure, as though she were eating a sweet)* Lapagaria. Sub-tropical. With waxy umbels.

MRS. ST. MAUGHAM. Lady Dorchester had it in her wedding bouquet after the Battle of the Marne! I had forgotten it! Could I grow it in my greenhouse?

MADRIGAL. *(By rote)* It needs the early actinic rays.

Exclude the sun again at midday. Counteract the high lime-content in your soil with potash.

MRS. ST. MAUGHAM. Where did you learn about such things?

MADRIGAL. I was put in charge of—

MRS. ST. MAUGHAM. What?

MADRIGAL. — a garden.

MAITLAND. *(Enters, carrying everything most correctly—liqueur bottle, two small glasses, silver tray, and even a clean napkin over his arm. Sets down tray. Then, straightening himself)* I wish to give my notice.

MRS. ST. MAUGHAM. *(Eyes like steel)* If I take it you will not get it back again.

MAITLAND. I am prepared for that.

MRS. ST. MAUGHAM. *(Terrible)* Are you?

MAITLAND. *(Immediately broken)* You know I can't stand criticism! Every time a word's said against me a month's work is undone!

MRS. ST. MAUGHAM. We all make mistakes.

MAITLAND. *(Passionately)* But nothing should be said about them! Praise is the only thing that brings to life again a man that's been destroyed! But oh if I leave— what will you do without me!

(Another SCREAM is heard from the garden.)

—and what will the child do! *(Runs off into the garden up Right.)*

MRS. ST. MAUGHAM. *(Smiling in triumph)* Do you know the secret of authority, Miss Madrigal? Changes of mood. The inexplicable. The thunder, the lightning, and the sudden sun. He won't leave me! Will you have a Crême de Menthe?

MADRIGAL. *(Stiffly)* I never touch alcohol.

MRS. ST. MAUGHAM. *(Filling glass)* Certainly he makes scenes. But I like them. He has been a prisoner.

MADRIGAL. *(Pause)* A prisoner!

MRS. ST. MAUGHAM. Five years. Now that there are no subject races, one must be served by the mad, the sick, and those who can't take their place in the outside world —and served I must be. *(Drinks.)*

(LAUREL *rushes in from the garden and stands looking out of the garden door up Right.*)
(Sees LAUREL) Laurel!

LAUREL. *(Not turning)* One moment, Grandloo. One
moment, darling— I'm watching the bonfire— I must see
it die— *(To Left of chair)* I put salt on it to turn the flame
blue. Blocks of it.

MRS. ST. MAUGHAM. *(Takes* LAUREL'S *hand)* Who told
you to put salt on it?

LAURA. The old bastard, Mr. Pinkbell.

MRS. ST. MAUGHAM. Not now, my darling. Superlatives
only between ourselves!

LAUREL. *(Looking at Left chairs)* Where are the others?

MRS. ST. MAUGHAM. *This* is Miss Madrigal!

LAUREL. Have you settled everything? *(To* MISS
MADRIGAL) Do you understand all about me?

MADRIGAL. Not yet.

LAUREL. Oh can't we have the interview together? Shall
I go and fetch the book that explains me?

MRS. ST. MAUGHAM. Not so fast. Externalize! Externalize, my darling! She has quaint self-delusions. You
mustn't mind them—

(MAITLAND *enters, with jacket over arm, from garden and
with a black look at* LAUREL *exits through his door.*)

LAUREL. *(Behind chair)* —but you mustn't cross them!
(Looks at MAITLAND *over left shoulder.)*

MADRIGAL. Are you an only child?

LAUREL. I am Delilah's daughter!

MRS. ST. MAUGHAM. Laura has a poltergeist! Stones
fall in the bedrooms, and words leap and change colour in
her mouth like fishes! I too at her age—

LAUREL. Wit often skips a generation!

MRS. ST. MAUGHAM. She is my parchment sheet on
which I write! I hope she will remember my life and times!
There seems no one else to do it—

LAUREL. *I* am your little immortality.

MRS. ST. MAUGHAM. *(To herself—with reality)* Those

who eat too big a meal of life—get no monument. You see how light my finger lies on her! The child's a flower. She grows in liberty!

MADRIGAL. Weeds grow as easily.

MRS. ST. MAUGHAM. As I was saying—

LAUREL. —before the interruption.

MRS. ST. MAUGHAM. Freedom is Captain here! Calm is its Lieutenant!

NURSE. *(Rushes in down Right. Leaves door open)* The madonna lilies have blown over!

MRS. ST. MAUGHAM. *(Rises)* Great heavens! This mule of a garden. Maitland!—He was to order the bamboos and he forgot them!—Are they all down?

NURSE. *(With triumph)* All. And not for want of warnings! *(Exits.)*

MRS. ST. MAUGHAM. Oh my lilies! My lilies! One waits a year for them!— *(Exiting fast into the garden.)*

(LAUREL *follows to Centre door.* MADRIGAL *to up Right door.)*

MAITLAND. *(Enters with two clean towels and a pair of shoes)* What was that I heard?

LAUREL. *(In Centre doorway)* The calm of Grandloo.

MAITLAND. *(Puts things on floor)* But what's happened?

MADRIGAL. There's been an accident in the garden.

MAITLAND. Fire!

LAUREL. *(To front of Left chairs)* Wind. You didn't stake the lilies!

MAITLAND. *(Frantic, rushing to the door to look out)* Oh are they down! The nurse told me and I forgot! *(Left of armchair)* How the old bastard will be crowing!

MADRIGAL. *(Up Right of armchair. Primly)* Stake in May.

MAITLAND. They weren't full grown in May!

MADRIGAL. They should have been.

MAITLAND. *(Fiercely)* Is that a criticism?

MADRIGAL. *(Quietly)* So you are the gardener here as well?

MAITLAND. *(Excited)* I'm everything! I'm the kingpin and the pivot and the manservant and the maidservant and the go-between, *(Turning on* LAUREL) and the fire-extinguisher!

LAUREL. Prisoner Six Five Seven Four!

MAITLAND. *(Jumping to attention)* Sir!

LAUREL. Carry your bed-area and about turn! Through the corridor second door on the left and into your cell! March!

MAITLAND. *(Marches to* LAUREL, *starts to salute, but can't quite make it)* I'm all to pieces. I can't play it.

LAUREL. *(Sitting third chair Left. To* MADRIGAL, *in mock-tragic tones)* He was five long years in prison, Miss Madrigal.

MADRIGAL. *(Politely)* Was it your first conviction?

MAITLAND. Conviction! It was for my ideals! I was a Conscientious Objector.

MADRIGAL. *(Prim)* And didn't you find it trying?

MAITLAND. She says "Trying!" Five years! Five long years! Given one chance to live and five years taken from it! An ant among a thousand ants—and taking orders from ants!

MADRIGAL. If it upsets you better not recall it.

MAITLAND. Not recall it! It's stamped on my skin and at the back of my eyes! It's in my legs when I walk up and down! In my heart that sticks with fright when *she* gets angry!

MADRIGAL. *(Sententious)* But since you felt you had right on your side!

MAITLAND. *(Moves* MADRIGAL's *macintosh on to her bag, then picks up first two chairs)* "Right on my side!" *That* didn't uphold me! *(To her with the chairs)* I went in there because I wouldn't take a life but before I came out I would have killed a warder! *(Takes chairs to hall —one behind curtain—other to Left of stairs.)*

MADRIGAL. *(Platitudinously)* All acts become possible.

MAITLAND. *(Over shoulder)* What can *you* know of life?

MADRIGAL. True, it's been sheltered.

LAUREL. *(Left of table, pours out a crême de menthe)* All our lives are sheltered.

MAITLAND. *(Turns and sees* LAUREL*)* Don't do that! She'll be furious! *(Rushes to her.)*

LAUREL. *(Tossing it down her throat before* MAITLAND *can reach her)* Not with me. I'm not responsible. *(Goes above* MADRIGAL *to behind sofa.)*

MAITLAND. *(To* MADRIGAL*)* You'll witness, Miss. I didn't touch it! I have to be on the ready for injustice in life!

LAUREL. *(Going below sofa)* From me? From your little Laurel? How touchy you are! *(Sits Centre of sofa.)*

MAITLAND. I have soft ground and hard ground to my feelings. You should mind where you step! *(To Left chairs.)*

LAUREL. *(Mock concern)* Have you taken your luminol?

MAITLAND. *(Putting* MADRIGAL's *bag close to up stage chair and macintosh over back of chair)* That's it! That's it! Even a child knows a man must take a sedative. But coming from you, Laurel—

LAUREL. *Miss* Laurel. I am a victim and you ought to love me.

MAITLAND. *(To Centre. Angrily)* I do love you—like the poor mother who ought by rights and reasons to take a stick to you. *(Crosses to stairs. Picks up towels and shoes.)*

LAUREL. What do you expect of me? A child that's been forsaken by its mother!

MAITLAND. That's as may be! That's as those think it to be! I was found in a field but I don't make a fuss about it! *(Rushes upstairs.)*

LAUREL. *(Soapily)* Poor Maitland likes the Right— even when the Right is wrong.

MADRIGAL. *(Platitudinous)* He has your interests at heart.

LAUREL. *(With interest)* Are you a hospital nurse?

MADRIGAL. Why do you ask?

LAUREL. You have that unmeaning way of saying things.

MADRIGAL. *(After a second's pause and with a little formal manner of adapting herself)* Now that we are alone —am I to call you Laurel?

LAUREL. *(Moves down stage on sofa)* It's my name.

MADRIGAL. *(Sitting beside her)* And what are you interested in—Laurel? I mean—apart from yourself?

LAUREL. What I don't like—is to be questioned.

MADRIGAL. I agree with you.

LAUREL. But I don't like to be agreed with—just in case I might argue! And I don't like to be read aloud to unless I suggest it! But if read aloud to—*I don't like emphasis!* And every morning I don't like *"Good* morning" said! I can see for myself what sort of a day it is!

MADRIGAL. You sound as if you had lady-companions before. How did you get rid of them?

LAUREL. I tell Pinkbell.

MADRIGAL. He tells your grandmother. My mind works more slowly than yours. But it was going that way.

LAUREL. You see she loves to advertise! She loves what comes out of it. It's like dredging in the sea, she says—so much comes up in the net!

MADRIGAL. I—for instance?

LAUREL. Why not?

MADRIGAL. Doesn't she take a chance—that way?

LAUREL. No, she says you get more out of life by *hap*-hazard. By the way, if you want to get on with my grandmother—you must notice her eccentricity.

MADRIGAL. She is fond of that?

LAUREL. She adores it! Oh, the tales I let her tell me when I am in the mood!

MADRIGAL. *(Pause)* Does she love you?

LAUREL. She would like to! *(Confidentially)* She *thinks* she does!—But I am only her remorse.

MADRIGAL. You try your foot upon the ice, don't you?

LAUREL. I find you wonderfully odd. Why do you come here?

MADRIGAL. I have to do something with my life—

LAUREL. What life have you been used to?

MADRIGAL. *(Softly)* Regularity. Punctuality. Early rising—

LAUREL. It sounds like a prison!

MADRIGAL. —and what are *you* used to?

LAUREL. Doing what I like. *(Rises behind sofa)* Have you been told *why* I am peculiar?

MADRIGAL. Something was said about it.

LAUREL. If you come here we'll talk for hours and hours about it! I'll tell you everything! And why I hate my mother!

MADRIGAL. I too hated my mother. I should say it was my stepmother.

LAUREL. Oh, that's just an ordinary hatred. Mine is more special.

MADRIGAL. The dangerous thing about hate is that it seems so reasonable.

LAUREL. Maitland won't let me say so, but my mother is Jezebel! She is so overloaded with sex that it sparkles! She is golden and striped—like something in the jungle!

MADRIGAL. You sound proud of her. Does she never come here?

LAUREL. *(Below armchair)* To see me? Never! She's too busy with love! Just now she's in Arabia with her para*mour!* *(Sits.)*

MADRIGAL. With her—?

LAUREL. If you pin me down he is my stepfather! Have you read Hamlet? It tipped my mind and turned me against my mother.

MADRIGAL. Does she know you feel discarded?

LAUREL. I don't. I left her! *(Pause)* The night before she married—she forgot to say goodnight to me— Does that sound a very little thing?

MADRIGAL. *(With sudden passion)* Oh no! It lights up everything.

LAUREL. *(Looking at her)* Are you talking of you? Or of me!

MADRIGAL. *(Her hand on breast)* When one feels strongly—it is always of me!

LAUREL. Oh, if you are not a spy sent by my mother, I shall enjoy you! Do you know about crime? Maitland and I share a crime library. Bit by bit we are collecting the Notable Trial Series.

MADRIGAL. *(Low)* Don't you like detective stories better?

LAUREL. No, we like real murder! The trials. We act the parts!

MADRIGAL. *(Faintly)* Which—trials have you got?

LAUREL. So far—only Mrs. Maybrick, Lizzie Borden, Dr. Crippen. But Maitland likes the murder*esses* better. He's half in love with them. Oh, if you come here—

MADRIGAL. Here!— *(Rises with gloves and handbag. Crosses Left Centre.)*

LAUREL. —couldn't we act them together? *(Gets no answer)* Maitland is so slow I make him read the prisoner. *(Rises. Passes below her to below Left chairs)* Why does the prisoner have so little to say? *(Waits)* —do you think?

(Pause—no answer.)

What a habit you have—haven't you—of not answering.

MADRIGAL. I made an answer.

LAUREL. Only to yourself, I think.

(MRS. ST. MAUGHAM enters up Right. She carries a sheaf of Madonna lilies—some with broken stems.)

MRS. ST. MAUGHAM. All gone!—All— Oh—when things are killed in my garden it upsets me—as when I read every day in the newspaper that my friends die! *(Comes Right of armchair to below it.)*

(MADRIGAL does not move, remains facing down Left.)

LAUREL. I should have thought as one got older one found death more natural. *(Sits lower of Left chairs.)*

MRS. ST. MAUGHAM. Natural! It's as though the gods

went rook-shooting when one was walking confident in the park of the world! and there are pangs and shots, and one may be for me! Natural!

MADRIGAL. *(Takes her macintosh and bag and goes towards the hall. As she goes)* That is why a garden is a good lesson—

MRS. ST. MAUGHAM. What?

MADRIGAL. *(Turns at step)* —so much dies in it. And so often. *(Up on second step.)*

MRS. ST. MAUGHAM. It's not a lesson I look for! Laurel, take Miss Madrigal into the garden.

(LAUREL *to hall below* MADRIGAL.)

MADRIGAL. I think I must be going.

MRS. ST. MAUGHAM. *(Below chair to Centre)* I want you to see the garden.

MADRIGAL. *(Nervous)* I'll write— I'll let you know—

MRS. ST. MAUGHAM. There is nothing to know yet!

MADRIGAL. I'd better not waste your time.

MRS. ST. MAUGHAM. And that great bag— *(Takes it)* No one will touch it here! *(She puts bag on up stage table.)*

(LAUREL *and* MADRIGAL *exit into garden, but* LAUREL *darts back.)*

LAUREL. *(Conspiratorially)* Grandloo—psst!—What do you think?

MRS. ST. MAUGHAM. I never allow myself to think. I have another method.

LAUREL. But—

MRS. ST. MAUGHAM. And while you are in the garden, listen to her! She knows her subject.

LAUREL. But shall you take her?

MRS. ST. MAUGHAM. Certainly not! But before she goes I want her opinion on the garden. *(Vanishes through* MAITLAND'S *door with lilies.)*

(LAUREL *exits to garden. Although the front door is open,*
OLIVIA *rings the bell.* MAITLAND *comes downstairs.
He carries a broom.*)

OLIVIA. *(Entering hall)* I didn't telephone, Maitland.
(Into the room) I thought it better just to come. How is
my mother?

*(One is just aware that she is pregnant. She wears light
travelling clothes, as from the East.)*

MAITLAND. *(Leans broom against banisters)* She has
the health of— *(Grasping for the unexplainable in Madam's health)* —something in Nature!
OLIVIA. And my daughter?
MAITLAND. They're as thick as thieves, Madam.
OLIVIA. Could you look for my mother—
MAITLAND. Madam was here. *(Takes broom and exits
to pantry, calling)* Madam!

(OLIVIA *moves to Right end of up stage table and puts
her handbag on it.* MADRIGAL *enters quickly from the
garden, making for her macintosh on chair in hall.*)

OLIVIA. *(As she enters)* Who are you?
MADRIGAL. *(Not looking at her)* It makes no difference.
*(Takes macintosh and goes up stage for bag. Suddenly
pausing)* Perhaps I should tell you—the field is free for
you— *(She does not pick up her bag.)*
OLIVIA. To see the child?
MADRIGAL. You have to see the grandmother first!
OLIVIA. *(Pause)* Yes.
MADRIGAL. Looking at you I wouldn't come here if
there is any other post open to you.
OLIVIA. Why?
MADRIGAL. Because the child will make hay of you!
OLIVIA. She *has* made hay of me!
MADRIGAL. Are you the mother?

OLIVIA. Yes. *(Looks towards up Right door)* Is she out there?

MADRIGAL. Yes.

OLIVIA. Please—go out—keep her there!

MADRIGAL. But I am a stranger.

OLIVIA. I know but sometimes one speaks the truth to a stranger. I'm not supposed to see her. First I must see my mother. *(Steps close to her)* Please, go out—

MRS. ST. MAUGHAM. *(From off stage)* Olivia!

OLIVIA. Please!

MRS. ST. MAUGHAM. *(Off stage)* Olivia!

(MADRIGAL *slips into garden.*)

(MRS. ST. MAUGHAM *enters from* MAITLAND'S *door. To* MAITLAND, *who has followed her into the hall)* Maitland —light a bonfire!

(He rushes off up Centre into the garden.)

Olivia! So soon! But you're safe—that's all that matters!

OLIVIA. Mother!—

(They embrace.)

MRS. ST. MAUGHAM. Oh—let me look at you! How brown you are! You look like an Arab. *(Brings her down stage)* How is the desert, darling? I can almost *see* the sand in your hair.

(OLIVIA *sits armchair.* MRS. ST. MAUGHAM *on sofa.)*

OLIVIA. Mother—how's the child?

MRS. ST. MAUGHAM. *(Stung)* Ask for *me*—ask for *me*, Olivia!

OLIVIA. I do, I would, but you ran in like a girl, and not a day older. As I came in—the standards dripping with roses. Oh the English flowers after the East!

MRS. ST. MAUGHAM. Let me tell you before we talk—

OLIVIA. —before we quarrel.

MRS. ST. MAUGHAM. No—not this time! I was going to say—that I've missed you. If I'd known you were coming I'd have driven up to see you. Whatever—and in your condition—made you rush down here without a word!

OLIVIA. I flew. I got here this morning.

MRS. ST. MAUGHAM. Like one of those crickets that leap from a distance and fall at one's feet! How do you do it?

OLIVIA. *(Gloves off)* By breakfasting in Baghdad and dining in Kuffra and taking a taxi in England. We're on a Course. I wrote. Two months at Aldershot.

MRS. ST. MAUGHAM. Aldershot! Oh—who would have thought you would have taken on that look—so quickly —of the Colonel's Lady! What is it they call it— Reveille? How are the bugles at dawn, Olivia?

OLIVIA. We don't live in a camp.

MRS. ST. MAUGHAM. I feel sure you said you did!

OLIVIA. Never mind the camp. I want to talk to you.

MRS. ST. MAUGHAM. But why down here the very second you arrive—and without warning!

OLIVIA. Mother, I've come about Laurel—don't put me off any longer.

MRS. ST. MAUGHAM. *(To distract from main issue)* Did you wear that scarf—on purpose to annoy me! What you wear is a language to me!

OLIVIA. *(Indignant)* That's an old battle—and an old method!

MRS. ST. MAUGHAM. When I've *told* you—in letter after letter.

OLIVIA. It's time I saw for myself, Mother! For nine years I shut the world out for her—

MRS. ST. MAUGHAM. *(Rises)* Nine years of widow-hood—might have been spent better! *(Above chair to Left of it)* I asked you *not* to come—but you *come!* I asked you to warn me—and you ignore it! And how can you wear beige with your skin that colour!

OLIVIA. Does it never become possible to talk as one grown woman to another!

MRS. ST. MAUGHAM. The gap's lessening! After fifty I haven't grown much wiser! *(Turns up Centre)* —but at least I know what the world has to have—though one cannot pass anything on! When I count my ambitions and what you have made of them!

OLIVIA. I did what you wanted—!

Mrs. St. Maugham. But *how* you resisted me! I was burning for you to cut ice in the world—yet you had to be *driven* out to gaiety! I had to beat you into beauty! You had to be lit—as one lights a lantern! Decked—like a May-tree—

Olivia. Oh, can't we be three minutes together—

Mrs. St. Maugham. *(Down stage again)* Even your wedding dress you wore like wrapping paper! And where is it now—the success to which I pushed you? Laurel might have been a child, these four years, playing in a high walled park— *(Sits upper chair Left.)*

Olivia. —and I might have been a widow, with deer gazing at me! But life isn't like that! You had for me the standards of another age. The standards of—Pinkbell.

Mrs. St. Maugham. Shy, plain, obstinate, silent. But I won. I married you.

Olivia. *(Rises. To her)* But you won't meet the man *I* married—the man *I* love!

Mrs. St. Maugham. Love can be had any day! Success is far harder.

Olivia. You say that off the top of your head—where you wore your tiara!

Mrs. St. Maugham. So you have found a tongue to speak with!

Olivia. I have found many things—and learned others. I have been warmed and praised and made to speak. Things come late to me. Love came late to me. Laurel was born in a kind of strange virginity. To have a child doesn't always make a mother. And you won't give up the image of me! Coltish—inept, dropping the china—picking up the pieces—

Mrs. St. Maugham. It was I who picked up the pieces, Olivia.

Olivia. *(Passionately) I know. But I'm without her.*

Mrs. St. Maugham. You are going to have another child!

Olivia. This child's the Unknown! Laurel's my daughter!

Mrs. St. Maugham. Who came to me—? *(Rises)* Who

ran to me—as an asylum from her mother! *(Crosses below her to armchair.)*

OLIVIA. *(Desperately)* Oh—you find such words to change things! You talk as if I were a light woman!

MRS. ST. MAUGHAM. *(Sits)* No, you are not light. You have never been a light woman. You are a dark, a mute woman. If there was lightness in you it was I who lent it to you! And all that I did—gone!

OLIVIA. *(Steps to her)* Mother! Of a thousand thousand rows between you and me—and this not, I know, the last one—be on my side! Oh—for once be on my side! Help me.

MRS. ST. MAUGHAM. To what?

OLIVIA. Help me to find her! Help me to take her back!

MRS. ST. MAUGHAM. Take her back! *(Lighting on an idea)* What, now?—Just now! When I've found such a companion for her! A woman of the highest character! Of vast experience! I have put myself out endlessly to find her!

OLIVIA. She can help you to prepare her. When I come back for her—

MRS. ST. MAUGHAM. You mean before the baby's born? That will be an odd moment—won't it—to come for her!

OLIVIA. *(Passionately)* No! It's *why* I want her! Before I love the baby! *(Crossing to sofa)* I can't sleep! I can't rest. I seem to myself to have abandoned her! *(Sits. Faces down stage.)*

MRS. ST. MAUGHAM. To her own grandmother! I am not a baby-farmer or a head-mistress or the matron of an orphanage—

OLIVIA. *(Turns on sofa)* But she'll be a woman! And I'll never have known her!

MRS. ST. MAUGHAM. It suited you when you first married that I should have her. Laurel came to me of her own free will and I have turned my old age into a nursery for her.

OLIVIA. *(With indignation)* And God has given you a second chance to be a mother!

MRS. ST. MAUGHAM. *(Rises)* Olivia!—Oh, there is no

one who puts me in a passion like you do! *(Crossing over to Left chairs with indignation.)*

OLIVIA. *(Rises)* And no one who knows you so well. And knows today is hopeless—

MADRIGAL. *(Enters from the garden up Centre on a high wave of indignation—matching the crescendo of the other two. Menacing—accusing—pulling on a glove)* Mrs. St. Maugham—there must be some *mistake! This* is a chalk garden! Who has tried to grow rhododendrons in a *chalk garden?*

MRS. ST. MAUGHAM. *(Taken aback)* Rhododendrons? We put them in last autumn. But they're unhappy! *(Sits. Picks up catalogue.)*

MADRIGAL. *(Magnificent, stern)* They are *dying.* They are in pure lime. Not so much as a little leaf-mould! There is no evidence of palliation! *(To upstage table for bag.)*

MRS. ST. MAUGHAM. Wait—wait— Where are you going?

MADRIGAL. *(Over her shoulder—going)* They could have had compost! But the compost-heap is stone-cold! Nothing in the world has been done for them.

(A gay SCREAM is heard from the garden.)

OLIVIA. *(To up Right. Looks towards garden. To MAD-RIGAL)* Is that Laurel? She's screaming. What's the matter?

MADRIGAL. *(Scornful)* There is nothing the matter! She is dancing round the bonfire with the manservant.

MRS. ST. MAUGHAM. I should have told you—this is Miss Madrigal. *(Opening catalogue)* Not so fast! I want to ask you—the bergamot—and the gunnera—

(OLIVIA takes handbag from up stage table.)

MADRIGAL. —won't thrive on chalk. *(Turns away to first step.)*

MRS. ST. MAUGHAM. There's an east slope I can grow nothing on.

MADRIGAL. —the soil can't give what it has not got. *(On to second step.)*

OLIVIA. *(Crossing to her)* Don't go! The wind blows from the sea here and growing things need protection!

MADRIGAL. *(Suddenly halted by the look on* OLIVIA's *face)* —and the lilies have rust—there is blackspot on the roses—and the child is screaming in the garden. . . .

MRS. ST. MAUGHAM. The roses! What would you have done for them! Pinkbell ordered—and I sprayed them!

MADRIGAL. *(Magnificent, contemptuous)* With *what,* I wonder! You had better have prayed for them!

(They measure each other for a moment.)
If you will accept me— *(Goes right up to her)* I will *take* this situation, Mrs. St. Maugham.

*(*OLIVIA *quietly exits.)*
(With a dry lightness) You have been very badly advised—I think—by Mr. Pinkbell.

CURTAIN FALLS

ACT TWO

Scene: *The same.*

A month or two later (to fit in with the flowers suitable to the garden—as mentioned in the text.)
About mid-morning.
The two chairs Left are now placed either side of the table in the window down Left. The drop-leaf table from the hall is now opened to its full circle, and stands down Left Centre. The armchair has not moved, but the small table beside it is now below the sofa. On it are the seed catalogue; a rose in a small vase; a glass jam-jar LAUREL *is using for her painting water, and a small cigarette box.*
LAUREL is seated on the sofa with an old mahogany box of water colours. She is painting the rose, in a painting book. Two other sheets of paintings are on the floor at her feet. She is now dressed in a linen frock and sandals.
MAITLAND enters carrying a large serving tray which he places on a console table which serves as a sideboard. He takes from sideboard a bottle of turpentine and a rag and starts to remove grease spots from table.

MAITLAND. All alone? Whose idea is that?
LAUREL. *(Does not look up)* The Boss's.
MAITLAND. And not even burning the curtains?
LAUREL. *(With dignity)* I am painting a flower.
MAITLAND. *(Rubbing)* Occupational therapy?
LAUREL. What was yours? Picking oakum?

42

MAITLAND. Who would think you were weak in the head? You've given up screaming.

LAUREL. My madness is older. It's too old for screaming.

MAITLAND. *(Glancing at her)* Why do you sham mad —dearest?

LAUREL. *(In surprise)* "Dearest"?

MAITLAND. Only in a sad sort of way—I have no dearest. *(Above table, puts bottle on floor.)*

LAUREL. You shouldn't be sorry for yourself. It unmans you.

MAITLAND. *(Polishing table)* It's better than being vain and in love with the glory of one's misfortune! But I'll say this for you! The Boss has changed you!

LAUREL. I'm her business and her vocation.

MAITLAND. Oh—who could imagine that a maiden lady could know so much about life!

LAUREL. She's no maiden lady! She might be anyone! Might she be a love child?

MAITLAND. That's enough now! *(Proceeds to lay table from tray on sideboard.)*

LAUREL. *(Rises to Centre)* How prudish you are! Look how she came to us—with nothing! A lady from a ship-wreck! Her brush is new and her dresses. No box of shells by *her* bed—no mirror backed with velvet— Oh— she's cut off her golden past like a fish's tail! She's had a life of passion!

MAITLAND. *(Moves Left of table to below it)* What words you use!

LAUREL. *(Above table to Left of it)* You have a set of words you keep in a cage. Does she get any letters? Do you spy on her?

MAITLAND. Who?

LAUREL. Our duke's daughter, our hired companion! *(Sits upper chair at window.)*

MAITLAND. *(Now Right of table)* If you are talking of *Miss* Madrigal she never gets a letter.

LAUREL. Don't you get a hint or a sound or sigh out of her?

MAITLAND. No. Do you?

LAUREL. With me she's on guard. I can't surprise or ambush her. She watches me.

MAITLAND. Whatever she does you're the better for it!

LAUREL. *(Crossing below table to sofa)* Mr. Pinkbell doesn't think so.

MAITLAND. Poison he is—but influential.

LAUREL. *(Looking at painting)* If you ask me rows are coming!

MAITLAND. *(Above table)* I don't ask you. You're too set up with yourself and pleased as a peacock to be the bone of contention.

LAUREL. *(Coming Centre)* She says he's the devil in charge. He's ordered rhododendrons. It took a lorry to deliver them.

MAITLAND. *(Turn to her)* What's that got to do with it?

LAUREL. The Boss reversed the labels. *(To sofa again)* She sent them back again. *(Picks up paint box.)*

MAITLAND. *(To table again)* Whew— I'm for Miss Madrigal! I've no mercy on him.

LAUREL. Poor Mr. Pinkbell!

MAITLAND. A man's no better when he's dying! *(Picks up turps bottle.)*

LAUREL. What's in that bottle?

MAITLAND. Turps. Turpentine.

LAUREL. *(Rises with paint box—crosses to him)* Give it to me. *(Back to sofa.)*

MAITLAND. *(He does)* How did she take our having a visitor to lunch? *(To sideboard for vase and bread.)*

LAUREL. I was to wear this clean frock. Otherwise nothing. *(Looking at it disdainfully)* Straight as an envelope. It looks so adolescent—and with a Judge coming. *(Sits sofa.)*

MAITLAND. How do I call him? *(Salt, pepper and butter on table.)*

LAUREL. A Judge is called m'lord.

MAITLAND. Oh—I wish I could see it!

LAUREL. What?

MAITLAND. *(Above Centre chair)* Him in his robes and his great wig and all that happens!

LAUREL. *(Rubbing inside paint box lid with turpentine rag)* How you dote on justice!

MAITLAND. It's the machinery and the magnificence! It's the grandness.

LAUREL. *(Sly)* In prison—was there a grandness?

MAITLAND. No, I was brought up from a cell and saw none of it.

MRS. ST. MAUGHAM. *(Enters from garden, up Centre, with some Sweet Williams)* Heavens, Maitland! Is this a morning for daydreams! The gold toothpicks— The green handled ivory knives—! *(Speaking half fantasy, half memory.)*

MAITLAND. Locked away.

MRS. ST. MAUGHAM.

    And the key of the Safe! It's years since
      I've seen it!
    We used to have celery with the Stilton—
      —and the Bristol finger bowls and the
      épergne—
      —and the sieve we served the Caraque on!—
      —and those glasses for the brandy—

MAITLAND. They broke.

MRS. ST. MAUGHAM. There was a gold cigar box that played a tune King Edward gave me—

LAUREL. *(Rises, steps in)* Is it gold? I used to keep a mouse in it!

MRS. ST. MAUGHAM. Go and get it! *(Above table, she puts flowers in vase.)*

(MAITLAND to sideboard for glasses.)

LAUREL. I can't remember where I put it— But isn't the man who's coming—*old?*

MRS. ST. MAUGHAM. Puppy?

LAUREL. The Judge!

MRS. ST. MAUGHAM. That's what I called him!

LAUREL. Can I wear—?

MRS. ST. MAUGHAM. Wear anything you like! I'm sick of white things and innocence!

> *(The NOISE of a cricket ball being hit is heard outside the down Left window. LAUREL below table to window, she stands on lower chair. MAITLAND is behind MRS. ST. MAUGHAM.)*

Oh! Are they playing out there with the hard ball again? Can you identify them?

LAUREL. The one with the bat is the fishmonger's son.

MAITLAND. How do *you* know?

LAUREL. *(Waving her hand)* He's looking at me.

MAITLAND. Get down now!

MRS. ST. MAUGHAM. Leave that to me, Maitland.

(The NOISE of the cricket bat and ball is heard again.)

LAUREL. *(Getting down)* It's time I looked at boys— or I won't get the hang of it. *(To sofa again.)*

MRS. ST. MAUGHAM. *(To window taking no notice)* Every summer—the boys with their cricket! Every summer a broken window!

MAITLAND. *(Above table, setting glasses)* Isn't it strange that *men* play *cricket!*

MRS. ST. MAUGHAM. *(Turning)* And you an Englishman!

MAITLAND. At the Orphanage we played Rounders.

MRS. ST. MAUGHAM. *(Dismissing the whole subject)* We shall want sherry before luncheon. Bring the sweet as well as the dry. *(Looking down at the table he has now laid)* And shouldn't there be two wine glasses to each person? *(Below table to Right of it.)*

MAITLAND. But there's only one *wine!*

MRS. ST. MAUGHAM. Put two. I forget the reason. And the spoons *outside* the knives, Maitland!

MAITLAND. *(Desperately)* You said the opposite last time!

MRS. ST. MAUGHAM. Never! *(Changes spoon and knife, then a doubt enters her mind)* Someone must know! *(Turns away below chair)* I shall ask Pinkbell.

LAUREL. Pinkbell is sulking.

(MAITLAND *to sideboard for small plates.*)

MRS. ST. MAUGHAM. Why?

LAUREL. *(Mocking)* He is full of jealous rage about his enemy.

MRS. ST. MAUGHAM. What again! And where is she now?

LAUREL. *(Mocking)* She is urging on the agapanthus lilies.

MRS. ST. MAUGHAM. She is *what?*

LAUREL. She is using diluted cow urine. One in seven.

MRS. ST. MAUGHAM. *(Going between chair and sofa)* Oh, I must go and see at once and watch how *that* is done! *(Quickly exits to garden, up Right.)*

LAUREL. *(Above sofa, with paint box—calling after her)* Keep behind the escallonia hedge! Every movement is watched! *(Turns to MAITLAND)* He sent the nurse this morning for the field glasses. Prisoner 6574!

MAITLAND. Sir! *(Two steps forward—salutes.)*

LAUREL. *(Front of sofa)* Do you know whose paint box this is?

MAITLAND. Yours.

LAUREL. No. Come and look at it. *(Sits sofa) She* lent it to me. The Boss. *(Pointing inside the lid, where she has been rubbing)*

(MAITLAND *kneels by her.*)

Can you see where the letters are that are burnt in the wood there? Look—under the black mark. Under the smear of paint. It is C.D.—

MAITLAND. And W. It is C.D.W.

(MADRIGAL *is seen coming from garden. She uses the boot-scraper outside door up Centre.*)

LAUREL. Take the turpentine! I don't want her to see it!

(MAITLAND *exits to pantry.* MADRIGAL *enters from*

the garden. She has a trug, a trowel, and notebook
and pencil. Wears left glove.)

Oh!—Grandloo has just this minute gone to look for you!
(Sits Centre chair, leaves paint box up stage end of sofa.)

MADRIGAL. *(In doorway)* I caught sight of her but I
thought it best that we should not be seen together.
(Trowel in basket—notebook out.)

LAUREL. She's head over heels with excitement about
our guest. Does one still mind when one is old—what men
think?

MADRIGAL. *(Writing)* One never *knows* when one is
old—for certain.

LAUREL. She calls him Puppy. I think she was once
his mistress.

MADRIGAL. Do you know that?

LAUREL. *(Casual)* No.

MADRIGAL. Then why do you say it?

LAUREL. Why does one say things? It's more fun!

(MAITLAND *enters with napkins.)*

MADRIGAL. If you pretend—and it's believed—where
are you? *(Notebook in trug, glove off; puts basket Right
end of up stage table.)*

LAUREL. *(Smiling)* Where am I?

MAITLAND. *(Above table)* Floating away. The only
hold we have on this world is the truth. Oh to think I'm
to feed him! A man who's got so much power!

LAUREL. We've never had a judge here before.

MADRIGAL. *(Turning sharply)* A judge? Is the visitor
that's coming a judge?

MAITLAND. He's here for the Courts. He's on Circuit.

MADRIGAL. What's his name?

MAITLAND. It's in the newspapers. But the old bastard's
got them. They are carried up to him. I only get to read
them on the doorstep.

LAUREL. We can talk to him of murder.

MADRIGAL. *(Apron on up stage table)* If you do that it
will be a want of tact. It will bore him. *(Coming to front*

of sofa) You and I will sit at a separate table for luncheon. Maitland will put us a small table here by the sofa.

MAITLAND. *(Turns)* Not two tables! Not with a guest! Oh—that can't be managed!

MADRIGAL. *(Swiftly changing her manner to one of treacherous interest)* You can manage anything! *(To him)* Tell us what surprise you've arranged for us. What are we going to eat?

MAITLAND. *(Last two napkins on plates. Still upset)* Fortnum's have sent the cold cooked chickens. *(But unable to resist)* I have carved them. I have ornamented them with mint leaves. There's a salad. And salad dressing.

MADRIGAL. Out of a bottle?

MAITLAND. Mrs. St. Maugham doesn't believe so.

MADRIGAL. The bottled is so *much* better—but one must never say so!

MAITLAND. *(Surveying the table)* Oh when I have something to do, something to create, everything is clear again!

MADRIGAL. You look ten years younger!

MAITLAND. Oh—if we had guests oftener! The sense of rising to something! *(Exits.)*

LAUREL. Poor Maitland. How you twist him round your finger! *(With a certain suspicious hostility)* Why do we sit separately from the guest, you and I?

MADRIGAL. It used to be done at luncheon—in the best houses.

LAUREL. Had *you* a life in them? *(Rises to her; sharp)* Who is C.D.W.?

MADRIGAL. *(Taken aback, silent. Then)* My married sister.

LAUREL. I thought you had been born unrelated.

MADRIGAL. Did you?

LAUREL. And now you have a sister.

MADRIGAL. Yes.

LAUREL. Suppose you were to drop down dead. To whom should we write?

MADRIGAL. I shall not drop down dead.

(The house TELEPHONE rings.)

LAUREL. *(Above sofa to phone; picks up receiver)* Pinkbell! In a rage! He has practically stung me. *(Listening a second, then puts receiver down and backs up to up stage table)* He asked for you! Would you be afraid to speak to him?

MADRIGAL. *(Passes below LAUREL)* Mr. Pinkbell? *(She flinches from receiver. Listens)* Yes, it is I, Miss Madrigal. *(Listens.)*

(MAITLAND *enters with tray, four glasses and glass cloth. He listens.)*

Ah—but on that I disagree. *(Waits)* The rhododendrons —*I* sent them back again. *(Listens) I* reversed the labels! And if I could I would reverse everything! And I may yet —we shall see!

No, I'm afraid on that you are wrong, Mr. Pinkbell. Your facts are wrong—also your deductions! Yes, and alas it is the wrong time of year to plant them. And the wrong soil. *(Listens)* Not at all. Don't *blame* yourself. Amateur gardeners very often make that mistake. *(Hangs up.)*

MAITLAND. *Blame* himself!

MADRIGAL. He made use of sarcasm. *(Crosses above chair to table.)*

(LAUREL *above armchair.)*

MAITLAND. *(Above table)* My God, you shall have two tables! You shall have three if you like! And the breast off both the chickens.

(NURSE *enters from* PINKBELL'S *door, glares at* MADRIGAL *and crosses out to the garden as the* OTHERS *watch in silence, passes between sofa and chair and exits up Right.)*

LAUREL. *(To up Right door and back)* He's sent the Nurse for Grandloo. Now there'll be ructions!

(MADRIGAL goes below table for things she had collected.)

MAITLAND. *(Two glasses on table)* And with the judge coming! In the newspapers they say it'll be a long trial. Why, Miss! Haven't you read it?

MADRIGAL. *(Now Right of table, puts plates, etc., on his tray, then two glasses)* Are all the glasses polished?

MAITLAND. D'you think—in Lewes prison —*(Tray on chair above window.)*

MADRIGAL. *(Gently)* There's a cloud on this one. *(Hands MAITLAND a glass.)*

MAITLAND. *(Taking glass from her and polishing it)* —this murderer, that's lying in his cell—

MADRIGAL. *(Change of voice)* No man is a murderer until he is tried!

MAITLAND. —does the Judge look at him?

MADRIGAL. The Judge never looks up. He seems to sleep. But it's the sleep of cruelty.

MAITLAND. *(Persisting)* —when he first *sees* the Judge—

MADRIGAL. Why do you think only of the Judge? It's the jury they work on.

MAITLAND. But it seems when you read about such trials, that it must be the Judge.

MADRIGAL. *(Fiercely)* Read more and you'll see it's neither. *(To herself)* But fate.

MAITLAND. How can that be?

MADRIGAL. Because, when it starts, there's no freewill any more.

MAITLAND. *(Earnestly)* But they work, don't they, to get at the truth?

MADRIGAL. Truth doesn't ring true in a Court of Law.

MAITLAND. What rings true then?

MADRIGAL. *(To herself—trancelike)* The likelihood. The probability. They work to make things fit together. *(Moving)* What the prisoner listens to there is not his life. It is the shape and shadow of his life. With the accidents of truth taken out of it. *(Shaking herself free from her trance)* Time is getting on, Maitland.

MAITLAND. *(Running to door)* Oh, what would that man in prison give to be as free as I! *(Exits.)*

LAUREL. *(To her)* So you've been to a trial?

MADRIGAL. *(Crosses down stage to sofa)* I did not say I hadn't.

LAUREL. *(Follows)* Why did you not say—when you know what store we both lay by it!

MADRIGAL. *(Picks up two paintings from floor, puts them on small table)* It may be I think you lay too much store by it.

LAUREL. *(Relaxing her tone and asking as though an ordinary light question)* How does one get in?

MADRIGAL. It's surprisingly easy. *(Sits sofa, takes paint box.)*

LAUREL. Was it a trial for murder?

MADRIGAL. *(Closing paint box)* It would have to be to satisfy you.

LAUREL. *Was* it a trial for murder? *(Sits above her on sofa.)*

MADRIGAL. Have you finished that flower?

LAUREL. *(Rises. Yawns)* As much as I can. I get tired of it. *(Pause)* In my house—at home—there were so many things to do. *(She takes small table behind sofa and puts it Right of armchair.)*

MADRIGAL. What was it like?

LAUREL. My home?

MADRIGAL. Yes.

LAUREL. *(Doodling on a piece of paper and speaking as though caught unaware)* There was a stream. And a Chinese bridge. And yew trees cut like horses. And a bell on the weather-vane, and a little wood called mine—

MADRIGAL. Who called it that?

LAUREL. *(Unwillingly moved)* She did—my mother. And when it was raining—we made an army of her cream pots and a battlefield of her dressing table— I used to thread her rings on safety pins—

MADRIGAL. *(Picks up drawing book)* Tomorrow I will light that candle in the green glass candlestick and you can try to paint that.

LAUREL. What—paint the flame!

MADRIGAL. Yes.

LAUREL. *(Doodling again)* I'm tired of fire, too, Boss.

MADRIGAL. *(As she notices* LAUREL *doodling)* Why do you sign your name a thousand times?

LAUREL. I am looking for which is me.

MADRIGAL. *(Moves up stage on sofa)* Shall we read?

LAUREL. *(Sits desk chair)* Oh, I don't want to read.

MADRIGAL. Let's play a game.

LAUREL. All right. *(With meaning)* A *guessing* game.

MADRIGAL. Very well. Do you know one?

LAUREL. *(Above armchair)* Maitland and I play one called "The Sky's the Limit."

MADRIGAL. How do you begin?

LAUREL. *(Putting cushion from chair on floor and sitting down opposite her)* We ask three questions each but if you pass one, I get a fourth.

MADRIGAL. What do we guess about?

LAUREL. Let's guess about each other. *(Full stop)* We are both mysterious.

MADRIGAL. *(Sententious)* The human heart *is* mysterious.

LAUREL. We don't know the first thing about each other, so there are so many things to ask.

MADRIGAL. But we mustn't go too fast. Or there will be nothing left to discover. Has it got to be the truth?

LAUREL. One can lie. But I get better and better at spotting lies. It's so dull playing with Maitland. He's so innocent.

(MADRIGAL *folds her hands and waits.)*

Now! First question— Are you a—*maiden* lady?

MADRIGAL. *(After a moment's reflection)* I can't answer that.

LAUREL. Why?

MADRIGAL. Because you throw the emphasis so oddly.

LAUREL. Right. You don't answer. So now I get an extra question. Are you living under an assumed name?

MADRIGAL. No.

LAUREL. Careful! I'm getting my lie-detector working. Do you take things here at their face value?

MADRIGAL. No.

LAUREL. Splendid! You're getting the idea!

MADRIGAL. *(Warningly)* This is to be your fourth question.

LAUREL. *(Rises to Centre, turns)* Yes. Yes. I must think —I must be careful. *(Shooting her question hard at MADRIGAL)* What is the full name of your married sister?

MADRIGAL. *(Covers paint box with hands; staring a brief second at her)* Clarissa Dalrymple Westerham.

LAUREL. Is Dalrymple Westerham a double name?

MADRIGAL. *(With ironical satisfaction)* You've *had* your questions.

LAUREL. *(Gaily accepting defeat)* Yes, I have. Now yours. You've only three unless I pass one. *(Sits on cushion again.)*

(Pause.)

MADRIGAL. Was your famous affair in Hyde Park on the night of your mother's marriage?

LAUREL. *(Wary)* About that time.

MADRIGAL. What was the charge by the police?

LAUREL. *(Wary)* The police didn't come into it.

MADRIGAL. Did someone follow you? And try to kiss you?

LAUREL. *(Off her guard)* Kiss me! It was a case of Criminal Assault!

MADRIGAL. *(Following that up)* How do you know— if there wasn't a charge by the police?

LAUREL. *(Pausing a second. Triumphant)* That's one too many questions! *Now* for the *deduction!* *(Cushion back on chair and sits.)*

MADRIGAL. You didn't tell me there was to be a deduction.

LAUREL. I forgot. It's the whole point. Mine's ready.

MADRIGAL. And what do you deduce?

LAUREL. *(Taking breath)* —That you've changed so

much you must have been something quite different. When you first came here you were like a rusty hinge that wanted oiling. You spoke to yourself out loud without knowing it. You had been *alone.* You may have been a missionary in Central Africa— You may have escaped from a private asylum— But as a maiden lady you are an impostor. *(Changing her tone slightly—slower and more penetrating)* About your assumed name I am not so sure— *But you have no married sister.*

MADRIGAL. *(Lightly)* You take my breath away.

LAUREL. *(Leaning back in chair; as lightly)* Good at it, aren't I?

MADRIGAL. Yes, for a mind under a cloud.

LAUREL. Now for your deduction!

MADRIGAL. Mine must keep. *(Rises with paint box, to down Right door.)*

LAUREL. But it's the game! Where are you going? *(Rises; steps down stage.)*

MADRIGAL. *(Pleasantly)* To my room. To make sure I have left no clues unlocked. *(Opens door.)*

LAUREL. To your past life?

MADRIGAL. Yes. You have given me so much warning. *(Exits down Right.)*

(LAUREL, *taken aback, stands a moment looking after her. Looks around room. Then takes the silver handbell from the table and rings it.*)

MAITLAND. *(Rushes in from his door, putting his jacket on)* Was it you! You're not supposed to ring it. *(Is about to go again.)*

LAUREL. Maitland!

MAITLAND. I'm busy now!— *(Going, but unable to go)* —Now what is it? *(To Left of table.)*

LAUREL. *(Conspiratorial)* The Boss! We played the game!

MAITLAND. *(Immediately caught)* You didn't dare! What did you ask her?

LAUREL. Nothing. And everything. No game would uncover her! But Maitland—*she knows about life!*

MAITLAND. What sort of knowledge?

LAUREL. Something—intense. Something too dreadful. Something cut in stone over her mind—to warn you when you walk in.

MAITLAND. *(Wistful)* I too had something dreadful happen to *me*.

LAUREL. *(Turns)* But hers is more dreadful! That's why she has no weakness. Her eyes see through me! I'm a mouse to her.

MAITLAND. *(To below table. Tenderly)* Are you afraid —poor dearest? Let Maitland speak to her.

LAUREL. *(Bidding for his co-operation)* You! Oh *you* tell her— How they brought me back that night—

MAITLAND. Don't talk of it!

LAUREL. So small, such a little thing! How I cried— They should have called a doctor.

MAITLAND. It's what I said they should! I argued it! Madam's got her ways! I've got mine! Oh—she would have got the moon for you! But I was the one who put up with you—who fetched and carried, who read to you. You had the right to the best in the world! A lady's child!—

LAUREL. *(Teasing)* "The Colonel's Lady."

MAITLAND. Not that again. *(Instantly furious)* I forbid you! Your own mother! *(Above table to tray.)*

LAUREL. *(To up Centre)* Mr. Pinkbell says "Judy O'Grady"—

MAITLAND. *(To her, with tray)* I'll have none of it! Out with the devil in you! For shame! And just when I was talking nicely to you!

LAUREL. But I've told you what she is—

MAITLAND. Not me you won't tell! That's got no mother! If your mother's black as soot you don't say so to me, girl!

LAUREL. I shall scream.

MAITLAND. Scream away! Now we've got the Boss to get after you! Oh, the relief of it! *(Away Left.)*

LAUREL. *(Quickly below, to Left of him. Pleading)* No! No—*be* nice to me! How tough you get—suddenly!

MAITLAND. It comes over me. The Right comes up in me. Like when they tried to make a soldier of me. All of a sudden I *see* how things should be!

(Enter MRS. ST. MAUGHAM *from garden up Right, carrying three tall stems of hollyhocks,* NURSE *following her.)*

MRS. ST. MAUGHAM. *(To* MAITLAND, *immediately undercutting his attitude)* Cut the stems three inches shorter. Put them in the blue Italian vase and three aspirins at the bottom—

   *(*LAUREL *moves above table.* MAITLAND *takes flowers lamely and crosses up to step. The door down Right opens and* MADRIGAL *appears.* MAITLAND *remains standing with the flowers in his arms.)*

Oh. Oh indeed! My ears are filled with poison! What has the nurse been telling me!

   (In silence the NURSE *exits down Right.)*

The poor old man upstairs is crying with rage!

MADRIGAL. *(Calmly)* I corrected him.

MRS. ST. MAUGHAM. *(Left of armchair to below it)* But for forty years Pinkbell has never been corrected! He is the butler who was the standard of all London!

MADRIGAL. Let him take his standard from the garden! I corrected his ignorance of detail, dates, fundamentals, application of manure. I spoke—not of his spoons and forks, *(Crossing to Centre)* but of his shallow knowledge of the laws of growth. You can leave the room, Maitland. *(Faces up stage.)*

MRS. ST. MAUGHAM. That should have been said by me! But—go, Maitland!

   (He exits hurriedly, with tray and flowers. LAUREL *Left of table to below it.)*

Now— *Now*, Miss Madrigal—this is a crisis!

MADRIGAL. *(Equally severe, majestic)* Yes. *Now* you have to make your decision.

MRS. ST. MAUGHAM. I! I have!

MADRIGAL. Now you have to choose between us.

(A moment's silence.)

(Then, taking a step towards MRS. ST. MAUGHAM—*with low ferocious accusation)* Is Mr. Pinkbell to let the moment pass—when one should layer the clematis? When the gladioli should be lifted? *(Advancing another step, menacingly)* Has anyone planted the winter aconites? And the pelargoniums? *Who* has taken cuttings? (MRS. ST. MAUGHAM *sits sofa. Pause. With mounting indignation)* And the red tobacco seed and the zinnias and the seeds of the white cosmos for next year? Do you wish—like an amateur—to buy them!

MRS. ST. MAUGHAM. *(In a faltering voice)* I—always have—bought them.

MADRIGAL. *(At the height of her passion)* If that is how you wish to live I can be no party to it! I cannot hold communication with minds brought up on bedding plants —bought at the greengrocer's—dying in shallow boxes! Out there every corner is crying aloud! Must I be dumb when you and I approach together the time of year when all next summer must stand or fall by us! *(To below sofa, turns)* Have you time—before death—to throw away season after season? *(Exits on a sweep.)*

MRS. ST. MAUGHAM. *(Sinking on a chair) What* have I let in here out of an advertisement!

LAUREL. *(To her)* Oh—we shall lose her, Grandloo! Don't sit there! Go after her! Oh think what she knows about the garden!

MRS. ST. MAUGHAM. I *am* thinking!

LAUREL. Oh— She'll go if she says she will! You don't want to lose her?

MRS. ST. MAUGHAM. For nothing on earth! I'd sooner strangle Pinkbell! But how is it to be *done!*

LAUREL. With a cord.

MRS. ST. MAUGHAM. How is the *reconciliation* to be done! And with a guest at luncheon!

LAUREL. Weave her in—as you say you used to do in

London. Promise her the earth— Promise her the garden!

MRS. ST. MAUGHAM. The garden—? *(A quick glance upwards to the ceiling. Rises to down Right door)* But— what am I to say to *him?*

LAUREL. *(Follows down stage)* You are not afraid of *him!*

MRS. ST. MAUGHAM. I have always— *(Opens door)* —always been afraid of Pinkbell. *(Exits.)*

(MAITLAND enters with vase and flowers.)

LAUREL. *(Taking vase from him and putting it on Right end of up stage table)* If we are to keep the Boss we must fight for her!

MAITLAND. Fight for her! Have you upset her? *(Sets chair from down Left at table for MRS. ST. MAUGHAM.)*

LAUREL. I haven't! Not I! She and I understand each other.

(DOORBELL is heard.)

There's the bell.

MAITLAND. *(Looks through down Left window)* The judge! *(Sets other chair for JUDGE and goes to front door.)*

(The JUDGE enters followed by MAITLAND.)

LAUREL. *(Radiantly)* Oh—the Judge! Oh—we're all expecting you! *(Comes forward and shakes hands.)*

JUDGE. *(Smiling)* All? *(Looks round—and sees only MAITLAND.)*

LAUREL. I am. And Maitland.

(MAITLAND makes a nervous gesture.)

Take his coat.

(MAITLAND jumps to it, puts cap and coat on up stage chair in hall.)

And my companion, Miss Madrigal. And my grandmother.

JUDGE. *(Crossing to below armchair)* So you're the grandchild?

LAUREL. Maitland, bring the sherry! The dry and the sweet, remember!

(MAITLAND *exits to pantry.*)

JUDGE. *(Sits armchair)* Not for me! I never drink at midday.

LAUREL. *(Left of him)* But my grandmother was telling me this morning you used to glory in your palate!

JUDGE. We change as we grow older. As you'll find, little girl!— *(Looking at her)* But she *isn't* a little girl!

LAUREL. I am sixteen. But backward.

JUDGE. Bless my soul! What am I to make of that!

LAUREL. Nothing. It's too long a story. *(Sits in chair Right of table.)*

JUDGE. So you are Olivia's daughter? Shy Olivia.

LAUREL. *(Finger on lips)* Hush. We don't speak of her.

JUDGE. She is living, I hope, my dear child?

LAUREL. In sin, Judge.

(Enter MRS. ST. MAUGHAM *down Right. The* JUDGE *rises.* LAUREL *rises.)*

MRS. ST. MAUGHAM. *(Coming in on a swirl)* So you've met her! The little girl of my little girl. No grandmother today! But *Puppy*—after twenty years— No longer *young!*

(JUDGE *kisses her hand.* LAUREL *sits again.*)

JUDGE. What do you expect when you measure me by that unsuitable nickname! Am I late? I lost my confounded way.

MRS. ST. MAUGHAM. But you don't drive yourself!

(MAITLAND *enters with sherry tray, which he puts on small table Right of armchair.*)

JUDGE. I do.

(MRS. ST. MAUGHAM *sits armchair.*)

I'm so poor. And much too old to be poor. *(Suddenly, snatching his handkerchief)* Oh—forgive me—

MRS. ST. MAUGHAM. *(Pouring sherry)* Have you a cold?

JUDGE. We won't pin it down! A trifle. An allergy. They were threshing in the cornfields. *(Sneezes. Puts on a large pair of dark sun spectacles)* I can stand London dust—but not the country!

LAUREL. But now we can't see you!

JUDGE. You will! Twenty minutes will cheat my old nose that we are back at the Old Bailey.

(MAITLAND *carries in tray with chicken, salad and wine in a cooler and sets on sideboard. He exits at once.* MRS. ST. MAUGHAM *offers sherry to* JUDGE, *who refuses it.*)

MRS. ST. MAUGHAM. Before we talk of the past—how do you find the present?

JUDGE. *(Going towards door up Right to look out)* Too busy. Too busy. One hasn't time to think one's getting nearer to God.

LAUREL. *(Whispers to her grandmother. Anxious)* Have you made it right with her?

MRS. ST. MAUGHAM. *(To* LAUREL*)* Speak louder. Never whisper. *(To* JUDGE*)* My Laurel has a companion. A charming woman. Able—but passionate. At war, just now, with Pinkbell.

LAUREL. *(Still anxious)* Grandloo—

MRS. ST. MAUGHAM. The door was closed, sweet. One is not at one's best through mahogany. But I heard no sound of packing.

JUDGE. *(Above sofa)* Pinkbell— What it brings back! What incorruptible ritual! How I remember—after the summer glare of Piccadilly—the young man that I was crossing your hall—like a pawn across a chess-board—
    (MAITLAND *enters with two dinner plates and glass cloth to wipe plates as he puts them on table.* MRS. ST. MAUGHAM *signs* LAUREL *to go and look for* MADRIGAL. LAUREL *rises but only goes up Centre as the*

JUDGE *continues.)*
—and how after the first and second footman—one ar-
rived at last at *Pinkbell. He* stood at the foot of the
stairs! The apprehension one had of his sour displeasure—
    MAITLAND. *(Moves up to* LAUREL. *Under his breath)*
Not him—he's not meaning! *(Lifting his chin slightly at
the ceiling.)*

*(*LAUREL *puts a finger to lips.* MAITLAND *exits hastily.)*

JUDGE. —his severity, his corklike dryness—later on,
when I had to rebuke the public Eye, I remembered Pinkbell. *(As though surprised at himself)* My demeanour on
the Bench *is* Pinkbell's!
    MAITLAND. *(Enters with butler's tray laid for two. He
places it. Ready to burst—drawing himself up and letting
out the words like an explosion)* Everything—now—is at
your service—Madam!
    MRS. ST. MAUGHAM. Simply. Simply. Times have
changed, Maitland!
        *(*LAUREL *goes above sofa. Down Right door opens
        and* MADRIGAL *appears.)*
Ah here she is!—our Miss Madrigal!
        *(*MADRIGAL *sweeps in, wrapt in an enigmatic mantle
        of silence, the temporary dressing gown of her anger
        and offence. Stands by bookcase, facing down stage.
        JUDGE to Left of chair.)*
Let me introduce you!
        *(*MADRIGAL *bows but without looking.)*
How you have relieved me! My right hand. My green
hand. The mistress of my garden. *(Slightly aside to the*
JUDGE) She has a specialty for the Anonymous! *(Louder)*
Some sherry—Miss Madrigal?
    MADRIGAL. No, thank you.
    MRS. ST. MAUGHAM. Then—shall we all sit down?
        *(*JUDGE *to Left of table.* MRS. ST. MAUGHAM *above
        it.* LAUREL *up stage for stool.* MAITLAND *sets butler's
        tray in front of armchair.* LAUREL *brings stool, which*

she sets below the butler's tray. MAITLAND *stands Left of armchair.)*

But why this segregation?

LAUREL. The Boss's orders.

JUDGE. *(To* LAUREL) Are you below the salt? Or are we?

LAUREL. *(Sitting on stool)* Miss Madrigal means this to be the schoolroom.

(MADRIGAL *comes below sofa and sits in armchair.* JUDGE *sits Left.)*

MRS. ST. MAUGHAM. She is so witty!—Now you can start, Maitland. You can give us your cold chicken. *(Sits Right. To* JUDGE) I don't entertain any more. The fight's over. Even the table is laid with fragments of forgotten ritual.

(MAITLAND *serves chicken to* MRS. ST. MAUGHAM *then to* JUDGE.)

JUDGE. Faith is handed down that way.

MRS. ST. MAUGHAM. When Pinkbell is dead we shall not know why we use two glasses for one bottle.

MAITLAND. *(Serving chicken to* JUDGE) And what about the wine, Ma'am?

LAUREL. The Judge doesn't drink.

MRS. ST. MAUGHAM. And I have such a bottle of Chablis on the ice for you!

(MAITLAND *serves chicken to* MADRIGAL *and* LAUREL.)

JUDGE. Alcohol in the middle of the day disperses the old brains I try to keep together.

LAUREL. But aren't *we* to have any!

MRS. ST. MAUGHAM. If we get flushed, Laurel, and too much at our ease—

LAUREL. I think that will be nice—

(MAITLAND to sideboard for salad.)

MRS. ST. MAUGHAM. The reverse, alas, is the truth. But bring it, Maitland. Bring the bottle. *(To MADRIGAL)* —and after lunch shall we show the Judge our roses? *(To JUDGE)* Miss Madrigal has soil-magic! *(Leaning over again to MISS MADRIGAL)* Things grow for you—during the night.

(MAITLAND serves MRS. ST. MAUGHAM with salad.)

LAUREL. *(As MADRIGAL doesn't answer)* You mustn't talk to us. We're invisible.
JUDGE. But you have ears?
LAUREL. *(Nodding)* We *over*hear.

(MAITLAND serves JUDGE with salad.)

MRS. ST. MAUGHAM. You'll overhear the flavour of the past. Life was full of great rules then. And we high women were terrible. Would you have youth back, Puppy?

(MAITLAND hands salad bowl to MADRIGAL. He then goes to sideboard and starts to open the wine.)

JUDGE. No. For a man youth isn't the triumph.
MRS. ST. MAUGHAM. I'd have it back if I could—even life's reverses! *(Turning direct to MADRIGAL)* Wouldn't you, Miss Madrigal?
MADRIGAL. *(High and sharp)* You have spilled the salt, Laurel.
MRS. ST. MAUGHAM. I was asking—do you think grief tastes more sharply than pleasure on the palate?
MADRIGAL. *(Startled)* I beg your pardon—
MRS. ST. MAUGHAM. You can do better than *that*, Miss Madrigal!
MADRIGAL. I have not the give and take— *(Into her plate)* —of ordinary conversation.

MRS. ST. MAUGHAM. Show it to me, Maitland.
(MAITLAND *shows bottle to her—corkscrew already in cork.*)
Now, open it.

(He takes it to the sideboard and removes the cork.)

JUDGE. In that case—after luncheon you'll have to let me close my eyes!

(MAITLAND *comes below* MRS. ST. MAUGHAM *and pours a little in her glass for her approval.*)

MRS. ST. MAUGHAM. What—sleep in the daytime!
JUDGE. That shocks you?
(MRS. ST. MAUGHAM *approves the wine.*)
In my job old age is part of the trappings!

(MAITLAND *fills the* JUDGE's *glass, and remains listening.*)

MRS. ST. MAUGHAM. One grows old—all the same.
JUDGE. Judges don't age. Time decorates them. You should come and hear me! Learned and crumpled like a rose-leaf of knowledge I snuffle and mumble. I sham deaf. I move into Court with the red glory of a dried saint carried in festival.
(MAITLAND *fills* MRS. ST. MAUGHAM's *glass.*)
By some manipulation my image bows right and left to the Sheriffs—
LAUREL. *(To* MAITLAND) Maitland—*this* is what you missed!

(MAITLAND, *behind* MRS. ST. MAUGHAM, *glances at* LAUREL.)

JUDGE. What?
LAUREL. Maitland and I want to know—
MRS. ST. MAUGHAM. *(Warningly)* And—Miss Madrigal? Talk is a partaking. Not a usurping.

LAUREL. But it's *Maitland* who collects the Notable Trial Series!

JUDGE. Maitland?

MAITLAND. *(Shamed)* Maitland is myself, m'lord.

LAUREL. We read them aloud together, and we are converting Miss Madrigal.

(MAITLAND, *still with bottle, takes salad bowl from Right table to sideboard and remains up stage listening.)*

JUDGE. Ah!

LAUREL. *(Rises, to down Centre)* But tell us, in plainer language, how you will enter Court tomorrow!

JUDGE. In ermine. In scarlet. With a full-bottomed wig. Magnificent! Seeing me now as I am— *(Taking off his sun-glasses)* You wouldn't know me! *(Puts sun-glasses away.)*

(A wine glass falls, broken, to the ground.)

MADRIGAL. Oh!

MRS. ST. MAUGHAM. What's the matter?

LAUREL. *(Crosses Right)* She broke the glass. *(Sits up stage end of sofa to pick up the pieces. Puts them on sherry tray.)*

MADRIGAL. My hand knocked it.

MRS. ST. MAUGHAM. Maitland will get you another. Another glass, please, Maitland.

MAITLAND. *(Gazing at the* JUDGE*)* There are no more on the sideboard.

MRS. ST. MAUGHAM. There are plenty in the pantry.

LAUREL. Oh—don't make him leave the room while the Judge is talking!

MRS. ST. MAUGHAM. I forgot! *(To* JUDGE*)* Maitland has been in prison, Puppy.

JUDGE. *(To* MAITLAND*)* Have you indeed?

MAITLAND. Five years, m'lord.

JUDGE. *(Blandly)* I hope not too unpleasant?

MAITLAND. It's given me a fascination and a horror, m'lord, if you can understand. A little stage-struck.

JUDGE. Dear me, I hope that's not the usual effect. It's supposed to be a deterrent.

MAITLAND. *(Waving the bottle wildly)* Yes and no. Yes and no. It's hard to explain—

MRS. ST. MAUGHAM. Don't try. Take my second glass and give some wine to Miss Madrigal. *(Hands glass to him.)*

LAUREL. When she had one she wasn't offered any.

MAITLAND. She doesn't drink, Madam.

MRS. ST. MAUGHAM. *(Conveying rebuke to MADRIGAL)* One's palate is reborn every morning! Fill the glass!

(He takes the extra glass to MADRIGAL.)

MADRIGAL. I am not used to wine—

MRS. ST. MAUGHAM. One must dissemble!

MADRIGAL. —but today I will have some.

(MAITLAND pours for MADRIGAL.)

MRS. ST. MAUGHAM. *(With meaning)* It helps one to hold up one's end—at a table.

LAUREL. *(Holding out her glass)* And mine! Fill mine! Oh Judge—go on!

(MAITLAND fills LAUREL's glass.)

JUDGE. With what?

LAUREL. With tomorrow. *(Drinks.)*

(MAITLAND stops to pick small bits of broken glass and to do so leaves bottle on MADRIGAL's table. From then on MADRIGAL fills her own glass from time to time.)

MRS. ST. MAUGHAM. Heavens, Laurel! Talk is a thoroughbred! One does not say "go on!"—as if it were a donkey!

(MAITLAND *exits with broken glass in wine napkin.*
LAUREL *moves down stage end of sofa.*)

JUDGE. First I am driven to church to pray.

LAUREL. To *pray!*

JUDGE. I pray against my faults. When you are as old
as I am and sit in a high place—everyone sees your faults
except yourself. I suspect I am vain. But I get no cor-
roboration. I have my likes and dislikes. Nobody should
know that—but everybody knows it.

LAUREL. The jury doesn't know it!

JUDGE. You are wrong. Once the battle around the
prisoner is ended—the relationship is between me and the
jury. *Then* comes the gamble! Wooden, inscrutable, as
they sit hour after hour—they grow a communal nose.
They sniff out weaknesses. I may speak seldom. But
there's no neutrality even in the rarest words. Even in
silence. Long, long before I come to sum up they have
taken mysterious sides for and against me. *(Picks up
knife and fork)* I pray against bias. And against vanity.

MADRIGAL. *(Low)* And—for charity?

(MRS. ST. MAUGHAM *takes her plate to the sideboard.*
MAITLAND *enters with cheese. He takes her plate. She
takes cheese dish.*)

JUDGE. *(Smiling)* That's outside my job. *(To* MADRI-
GAL) I am sorry— I have forgotten how they call you?

MADRIGAL. The name is Madrigal. *(Pours wine.)*

JUDGE. *(Finishes with his plate)* I ignore the heart,
Miss Madrigal, and satisfy justice. *(To* MRS. ST.
MAUGHAM *on her return)* Every little line on my face is
written by law, not life.

MRS. ST. MAUGHAM. *(Comes above table with cheese)*
Oh—to be bound up again, Puppy! as you are! To be
involved—to be back in the hurly-burly—

(MAITLAND *collects the two plates Right, then* JUDGE'S
plate and exits with them.)

JUDGE. My life's not the hurly-burly! That's for the Counsel!

(MRS. ST. MAUGHAM *sits again.*)

I'm the old creature with the memory! I have to remember the things they *said* they said—but didn't. I have to decide according to dry facts—when appealed to in a passion.

LAUREL. *(Brings stool below* JUDGE *and sits)* But tomorrow, Judge! Tomorrow!

MRS. ST. MAUGHAM. Stop badgering the Judge, Laurel!

JUDGE. *(Indulgently)* No! Let her be! On to the Law Courts! At the gates my trumpeters knock three times. Then blow for my admittance. In a little room behind the court I change my great wig for a small one.

(MAITLAND *enters with sweets in a silver bowl. Puts them on table and stays to listen.*)

LAUREL. *(Breathless)* Then—?

JUDGE. *(Histrionic for her amusement. Slow and majestic—so that every word tells on* MADRIGAL*)* Then— garbed and toffed with medieval meanings, obscured by ritual, carrying the gloves of justice and the cap of death —on a hollow knock—I go in.

LAUREL. —and the prisoner—

(Exit MAITLAND. MADRIGAL *pours wine and drinks.)*

MRS. ST. MAUGHAM. Heavens, Laurel, after a speech like that you should have paused and clapped him!

(JUDGE *takes cheese, butter, biscuit.)*

LAUREL. But I want to ask a question!

MRS. ST. MAUGHAM. Not yet! I am trying to weave in. —Oh whoever invented two tables! Can't we join them?

JUDGE. Not across fifty years. Not the past and the present!

LAUREL. But can I ask the Judge—

MRS. ST. MAUGHAM. *Ask* then! But don't leave our friend out of everything!

(MADRIGAL *drinks.*)

LAUREL. *(Rises, behind* JUDGE *to above table)* I don't know how to *include* her—when I want to ask my *own* question!

MRS. ST. MAUGHAM. Ask Miss Madrigal—

LAUREL. But it's the *Judge* I'm asking! Judge—aren't you going to try a murderer tomorrow?

JUDGE. *(Suddenly grim)* That is not a subject for discussion.

MRS. ST. MAUGHAM. You see! You see how stiff he can be! You see the resemblance!

JUDGE. To whom?

MRS. ST. MAUGHAM. *(Delighted)* To Pinkbell!

(MADRIGAL *drinks.*)

LAUREL. *(To behind* JUDGE) But here, today, you are alone with us! No one will quote you! *(Pleadingly)* And we are mad on murder!

JUDGE. Murder is a sordid thing.

(MADRIGAL *pours more wine.*)

LAUREL. Oh—you don't think so! Murder cracks open the lives of people you don't know—like cracking open a walnut! Murder is a crisis! *What* must have gone before to make it so! Isn't it true that to you, Judge, everything is told for the first time?

JUDGE. In principle.

LAUREL. But Miss Madrigal says that the Judge isn't even interested! That he sleeps.

MADRIGAL. I said he *seemed* to sleep.

JUDGE. With one eye open. Like a tiger.

MRS. ST. MAUGHAM. *(To* MADRIGAL) Have you been to a trial, then?

LAUREL. She has. She told me.

MRS. ST. MAUGHAM. You defeat my purpose! Let *her* answer.

(LAUREL *sits on stool.*)

JUDGES. *(To* MADRIGAL, *politely)* Have you heard me in Court, Miss Madrigal?

MADRIGAL. When I spoke to Laurel of judges it was in a general sense. *(Drinks)* But I heard you on the Bench, Judge.

JUDGE. I trust it was one of my better days.

MADRIGAL. *(After a pause—ironic—and high with wine and danger)* I think, if I remember—I would not have come to your conclusion. *(Drinks.)*

MRS. ST. MAUGHAM. *(To* JUDGE) Miss Madrigal has such answers to life! *(To* MADRIGAL, *in quite a different tone, annoyed)* But *that* was a strange one!

JUDGE. Well, a judge does not always get to the bottom of a case. *(Drinks.)*

MADRIGAL. *(Loud)* No. It takes the pity of God to get to the bottom of things.

(Enter MAITLAND.)

MRS. ST. MAUGHAM. *(Rises)* That's enough! *(To a small table for cigarettes.)*

MADRIGAL. *(Over-riding)* Forgive me. *(Picks up bottle)* You insisted! It has removed the inhibitions. *(Pours wine.)*

(MAITLAND *takes* MRS. ST. MAUGHAM'S *plate.*)

MRS. ST. MAUGHAM. *(Loud) Bring the coffee on!*

(JUDGE *rises to* MRS. ST. MAUGHAM. MAITLAND *takes his plate and exits.*)

LAUREL. *(Rises. To* JUDGE) When it's a murderer—

what do you feel? *(Takes matches, goes Left of table to behind* JUDGE.)

MRS. ST. MAUGHAM. *(Hands* JUDGE *cigarette, then to Left of table with box)* What should he feel, Laurel! Judges see prisoners by the million!

LAUREL. *(Now Right of* JUDGE) But you've got to say, haven't you, whether the man's to live or die? Do you suffer? *(Strikes match.)*

(MRS. ST. MAUGHAM *sits Left of table.)*

MADRIGAL. *(Wildly, inconsequentially)* Nobody will suffer. They all go into a dream together!

LAUREL. *(Turns to* MADRIGAL) Even the prisoner?

(JUDGE *passes behind* LAUREL *to sit Right of table.)*

MADRIGAL. *(With an air of reasonable explanation)* The prisoner *thinks* he is at the judgment seat of justice, a place where all motives are taken into account.

LAUREL. And isn't it?

MADRIGAL. *(Loudly) No. (Drinks.)*

(MRS. ST. MAUGHAM *rings the handbell.)*

LAUREL. *(Comes above table, puts matches down)* But Judge, while he listens—if the truth is quite different—does he never cry out?

JUDGE. He may write notes to his counsel.

LAUREL. *(Takes a sweet)* Miss Madrigal says that when all has gone against him—

MADRIGAL. I am quoted enough!

LAUREL. —that after the verdict—

MADRIGAL. *(With a sudden drunken desire for accuracy)* But if quoted, quoted rightly—

LAUREL. —when he is asked "Have you anything to say?"—

MADRIGAL. The prisoner is punch-drunk. And says nothing.

(Enter MAITLAND *with coffee tray, comes below* MRS. ST. MAUGHAM *to put it before her.)*

JUDGE. Not always. Some have said remarkable things. There comes to my mind a woman— Have you the trial, Maitland, of Connie Dolly Wallis?

LAUREL. Of whom?

MAITLAND. *(Stammering)* I—I haven't all the volumes, m'lord. I haven't that one.

JUDGE. It was not one of my successes. But you should read it for what the woman said when she stood before me. It was just before I sentenced her. *(Fingering his chin thoughtfully with his fingers)* Fine eyes she had. I think I should remember them. A tall woman. With a face like an eagle. "What I have been listening to in Court," she said, "is not my life. It is the shape and shadow of my life. With the accidents of truth taken out of it." Fifteen years ago it must have been. It was my sixtieth birthday.

LAUREL. What was she tried for, Judge?

JUDGE. Murder.

MADRIGAL. *(Suddenly)* I remember the case. *(Looking at the* JUDGE*)* A liar! A liar! *(Going high with the increasing combination of danger and wine)* A girl who lied and lied! And when she told the truth it didn't save her!

JUDGE. *(Looking at her, frowning, reminded of something, but baffled)* Have you been to many trials?

MADRIGAL. *(Gets up with an instinct to escape, which carries her no further than the sofa)* One trial. One. But it isn't the *duplication* that makes the impression! It's the first time—the first time—the first time—

(Crash! A cricket ball breaks a window offstage.)

MRS. ST. MAUGHAM. *(Still at table)* Quick, Maitland! It's the fishmonger's boy!—the fishmonger's boy! See See if you can catch him!

*(*MAITLAND *rushes out of the hall door.* MRS. ST. MAUGHAM *crosses to pour out the coffee.)*

LAUREL. (*To* JUDGE, *but with an awed glance at* MADRIGAL) *Was she hung?*

MRS. ST. MAUGHAM. (*Handing coffee cup to* LAUREL *to pass*) Hanged—my darling—when speaking of a *lady*.

CURTAIN

ACT THREE

Twenty minutes after luncheon.

> *The luncheon table is now back in the hall. The two
> chairs from it, back either side of window table down
> Left. The armchair is Left Centre with the small
> table Right of it. A cup of coffee and the seed cata-
> logue are on the table. The door up Centre is closed,
> The blind to the down Left window is down, and a
> light garden awning has been drawn outside garden
> window.*
>
> > *The* JUDGE *sits in the armchair, covers his face
> > with his handkerchief, pretending to be asleep.*
> >
> > LAUREL *enters from the pantry.*

LAUREL. *(To Right of him)* Judge—Judge—wake up—
(JUDGE *mumbles behind his handkerchief.)*
If you have your teeth out I will turn my back. *(Turns
her back.)*

JUDGE. *(Whipping off his handkerchief)* My teeth are
my own, thank God!

LAUREL. *(Turning again)* What have you been thinking of—under that handkerchief?

JUDGE. I am an old man—trying to sleep, Laurel.

LAUREL. *(Above chair to Left of him. Urgent)* What
did she *do?*

JUDGE. Who?

LAUREL. In that case you were speaking of.

JUDGE. In my day young girls didn't pester old judges
about murder.

LAUREL. You are old-fashioned.

JUDGE. You will be old-fashioned one day. It's more shocking than getting old. *(Pushes stool Left with foot.)*

LAUREL. Who died—that they should arrest her?

JUDGE. Her step-sister.

LAUREL. *(Moves stool close to Left of chair)* How was it done? And why? Was it jealousy? *(Sits stool.)*

JUDGE. *(Struggling to his feet and moving away Right)* If you are going to sit down I am going to stand up.

LAUREL. Was she hung?

JUDGE. *(Half turns)* Who? What are you saying?

LAUREL. *(Rises to him. Smoothly)* I was asking you about the case you were mentioning.

JUDGE. *(Shortly)* She was reprieved. There was a doubt.

LAUREL. Yours?

JUDGE. *(As shortly)* Not mine. *(To above sofa)* Enough has been said, I think.

LAUREL. *(Follows behind him)* Where do they go when they come out—all your murderers—when they don't go to the gallows?

JUDGE. *(Turns)* One doesn't—mercifully—know.

LAUREL. Do you remember them?

JUDGE. In some strange way they are catalogued. As I get older they don't always come to hand.

LAUREL. But one *would* know them—by peculiar habits?

JUDGE. Perhaps. *(Turns up to window)* Some mark might lie upon them.

LAUREL. *(To Right of him)* If they took their country walks, for instance, back and forth, up and down, wearing out the carpet in their bedroom—

JUDGE. What?

LAUREL. With a habit, like a sailor's, of walking in a confined space. Might it be *that,* Judge?

MRS. ST. MAUGHAM. *(Enters down stairs)* Laurel! He was to sleep, child! And now you have disturbed him.

LAUREL. *(To door up Right—looks back with a sly smile)* I think he was disturbed already! *(Exits to garden.)*

MRS. ST. MAUGHAM. My Original!—so elegant and gentle— What do you think of her?

JUDGE. *(To Right of table)* I am not fond of young girls.

MRS. ST. MAUGHAM. You are not? You used to be! *(To window table for writing pad)* It was unfortunate about her companion. But your fault, Puppy, for not drinking the wine at luncheon!

JUDGE. *(Below chair)* How did you discover her?

MRS. ST. MAUGHAM. I advertised. I took a chance and was justified. Miss Madrigal came to me like rain from heaven.

JUDGE. With references?

MRS. ST. MAUGHAM. I never listen to what one woman says of another. References are a want of faith—in one's own judgment! Finish your sleep, Puppy! Since you must have it!

(As MRS. ST. MAUGHAM *exits,* MADRIGAL *appears at the garden windows. Seeing the* JUDGE *alone she comes into the room. Crosses herself as she comes in.)*

MADRIGAL. I am sorry to disturb you. . . .

JUDGE. *(Wary, playing for time, needing the last link)* On the contrary—on the contrary— *(Waving his small silver box)* Old men are kept alive on tablets—

MADRIGAL. *(Attempting to control herself and speak reasonably)* Of course you think—this is not where I ought to be— There would be no difficulty— I have private means— But it's an understandable job. So fitted to me. *(Control going)* Do you believe in God? I thought God had given it to me!

(Pause. He says nothing.)

Oh—don't look at me as if I were a sad piece of news! A curiosity!

(Silence.)

(In agony) Why don't you *say* something!

JUDGE. *(With a sudden crack of his fingers—everything has cleared)* That's it!

MADRIGAL. *(Stopping short)* What?

JUDGE. Well—it has come to me.

MADRIGAL. Oh God— I thought you knew!

JUDGE. *(Still to himself)* I must say—the coincidences at luncheon—in retrospect—are distasteful.

MADRIGAL. *(Aghast)* If I hadn't come in. . . .

(Pause. He makes a wry little gesture.)

So . . . *now* what will you do?

JUDGE. I am an old man, Miss Madrigal, and very learned. I don't know.

MADRIGAL. *(Ironically)* Judge—I can't wait seven hours—twice! You sent me to meet my Maker on a Tuesday—but that was altered. I have done what they call "time." It was a lifetime. I don't know what you *can* do to me! *What* can you do to me?

JUDGE. I do not presume to judge you twice.

MADRIGAL. Oh, you would come to the same conclusion! Cleverer minds than mine could not convince you! But there's nothing to gain by talking! You came here by accident. . . .

JUDGE. I wish I hadn't.

MADRIGAL. *(Bitterly)* What can it be to you?

JUDGE. Embarrassment. What in the name of heaven made you choose *this* occupation! With your history! In this family!

MADRIGAL. *(Satirical)* In "this" family?

JUDGE. *(Testy)* In *any* family. I remember the young woman! And the lies she told. A Pathological Imaginer.

MADRIGAL. One does not forget the plums in one's speeches!

JUDGE. And now you have planted me—with ethical perplexity! It's most unpleasant.

. . . And *human* perplexity! Old friends . . . and a child to consider!

MADRIGAL. It's the child I'm considering! When I came here I thought I had met myself again. The cobwebs and the fantasies! The same evasions! I could have slipped away. . . .

JUDGE. There are worse solutions.

MADRIGAL. But the child needs me! *If* I stay—will you tell them who I am?

JUDGE. Connie Dolly Wallis—what the devil am I to do with you?

MADRIGAL. The name is Madrigal.

JUDGE. *(Testy)* Of course you had to take a name!

MADRIGAL. It's more than a name to me!

I come of a stock—who in some insensate way—*cannot* accept defeat!

My father was cashiered. And after forty years of appeals—re-instated.

My grandfather died upright on his feet.

He said God wouldn't give a fallen general houseroom.

For fifteen years, and alone, I have hammered out what I am.

I did not know I was as dogged as any of them.

JUDGE. But even conceding . . .

MADRIGAL. You need concede nothing to solitude! It is a teacher!

JUDGE. You were a girl of considerable feeling, if I remember.

MADRIGAL. Not now. I am burnt out white—like the moon—lunar.

JUDGE. Are you not—if I may gently say so—somewhat a stranger to life?

MADRIGAL. The girl I was! *She* was the stranger!

JUDGE. You have greatly changed.

MADRIGAL. *(Ironical)* At our last meeting I died. It alters the appearance.

JUDGE. *(Suddenly sorry for himself)* Dear me. . . . Oh dreary me. . . . As if there were not quite enough—this week ahead of me.

MADRIGAL. You would have been going. Why not leave?

JUDGE. Because I belong to a guild of men—who feel responsibility. *(Wryly)* And a deep distaste for situations.

MADRIGAL. What shall you do?

JUDGE. Don't badger me! I can't remember when I was so bothered! *(Sharply—as she puts her hand to her head)* What's the matter?

MADRIGAL. It is that . . . after being so long unknown . . . it makes my head swim to be known. . . .

(OLIVIA *enters from front door.* MADRIGAL *rises.*)

OLIVIA. *(Shakes hands)* Judge! I remember you! You used to be so kind to me when I was little! What was that odd name Mother had for you? Puppy? I used to wonder at it.

JUDGE. *(Smiling, taking her hand)* You were that silent little girl.

(MADRIGAL *crosses down Right.*)

OLIVIA. Yes, I was silent. *(She crosses after* MADRIGAL, *who pauses below the sofa)* We met before. Do you remember?

(They shake hands.)

I have come back, as I said I would, to fetch my daughter.

MADRIGAL. To *fetch* her?

JUDGE. *(Quickly intervening. Above sofa)* I have to go—can my car be of use, Miss Madrigal? *(Low)* It would be simple.

OLIVIA. *(Turns up to him)* Oh don't go—don't go! I'm so glad you are here! It's so lucky.

JUDGE. Lucky?

OLIVIA. For me. For with you here I shall put things better.

JUDGE. *(With his own special wry humour)* I ought to go. I am not good out of my setting.

OLIVIA. Surely *you* are not afraid of life?

JUDGE. On the contrary—the Law has made me nervous of life.

OLIVIA. No, Judge! Please stay! It's the influence of a stranger! With a third person in the room my mother hears reason better.

MRS. ST. MAUGHAM. *(Coming down stairs—catapulting into room)* Don't count on it, Olivia! *(Forestallingly)* I got your letter!

OLIVIA. But you don't read them. You never did!

(Crosses to her) We've had our orders. We leave tonight for Suez.

MRS. ST. MAUGHAM. Suez! Whoever heard of it! It flashed in history and is gone forever! *(To down Left window)* Disraeli—Bismarck—I can't remember! See what comes of marrying an Army officer? *(She raises the blind.)*

LAUREL. *(Makes her entry from the garden up Centre. Stands in entry, silent)* Have you come alone?

OLIVIA. Laurel!

(LAUREL goes to front of sofa.)

MRS. ST. MAUGHAM. We have a guest! No drama!

LAUREL. *(Turns)* You haven't been for four years.

OLIVIA. *(Glancing first at her mother in silent accusation. Right of chair to her)* But *now* I have come for you! Oh—as I drove down here—all the hedges and the telegraph posts were saying—Laurel—

LAUREL. Are you going to have a baby?

OLIVIA. Yes.

LAUREL. *(Sitting down stage end of sofa)* So there's no room for me!

(JUDGE above desk chair—looking Right.)

OLIVIA. There's room! There's always been room! A heart isn't a house—with a room for each person! *(To MRS. ST. MAUGHAM)* I can't wait any longer! *(To LAUREL)* Come just as you are—

MADRIGAL. *(Suddenly throwing her weight on the mother's side)* I can pack her things!

LAUREL. *(Turning on her)* What are you up to, Boss!

MRS. ST. MAUGHAM. *(Coming forward)* You are so kind! But there's no need for packing! *(Sits Centre chair.)*

LAUREL. *(Menacing. To MADRIGAL)* Did you speak without thinking?

MADRIGAL. No.

LAUREL. But I've told you what she is! I've told you—
MADRIGAL. And do you think I have believed you?
OLIVIA. There's a seat taken on the plane tonight—
LAUREL. *(Furious—but with* MADRIGAL) And fly with
you? Have you thought of the risk?
OLIVIA. On the plane? One doesn't think of that.
LAUREL. The risk that—if you take me— *(Looks front)*
I might murder my step-sister!
JUDGE. Are you mad?

(OLIVIA, *turning to look at her mother, clears above
table.)*

LAUREL. *(Not looking)* They say so.
MADRIGAL. *(To* JUDGE) Don't give her the triumph of
your attention.
MRS. ST. MAUGHAM. Laurel always uses wild words
instead of weeping! *(To* OLIVIA) I knew that if she saw
you we should have trouble with her!
MADRIGAL. *(Quietly)* You have missed your effect,
Laurel— The moment is passing. Would you care to let
it go?
LAUREL. *(Menacing)* The sky's the limit, Boss! The
sky's the limit!
MADRIGAL. No time for games.
LAUREL. I mean—no limit! I can say anything!
JUDGE. I would not.
LAUREL. Shall I go on?
JUDGE. No.
LAUREL. Shall I?
MADRIGAL. If you want your scene—take it.
LAUREL. How calm you are!
MRS. ST. MAUGHAM. Miss Madrigal has the calm of a
woman in a million!
LAUREL. She has the calm of a woman who has been a
long time—alone.
MADRIGAL. *(Low)* So we are in for it?
LAUREL. No. It can be played on the edge still.

MADRIGAL. An edge is sharp! One has to come down one side or the other—!

MRS. ST. MAUGHAM. You see—they are always at some amusing invention! They're inseparable! What game, my poppet?

LAUREL. A game that two can play at.

(MAITLAND *enters from pantry with an empty tray. Comes to table down Left.* JUDGE *sits at desk.*)

Maitland! Look! It's my mother!

MAITLAND. I know it's your mother.

MRS. ST. MAUGHAM. Must the whole house be gathered!

MAITLAND. I came for the coffee cups. *(Takes cup from down Left table. Then goes above chair for other cup on small table.)*

MRS. ST. MAUGHAM. Oh no you didn't! You came for curiosity! You've a nose for a crisis like a basset for a wild hare!

(MAITLAND *is going.*)

LAUREL. *(Rises, crosses down stage to him)* Maitland! Wait, Maitland! *(On first step)* How did you know?

MAITLAND. She has been before—

LAUREL. How deep you are! *(To* MRS. ST. MAUGHAM *—below stool)* I did not know that.

MAITLAND. —But I am loyal to Madam! *(Exits quickly.)*

MRS. ST. MAUGHAM. *(Furious)* Loyal! Loyalty died with Queeen Victoria!

(OLIVIA *turns away.*)

Disregarded in my own house! Disregarded! I am talking to *you*, Olivia.

OLIVIA. *(Turns)* Each time I came you promised you would tell her.

MRS. ST. MAUGHAM. I had my own reasons! You never would listen! You were never like other girls! The Judge will remember—though daughters forget everything. You remember, Puppy, how I tried with her?

JUDGE. I remember only the result. The shy and gentle daughter.

OLIVIA. Thank you, Judge. *(To* MRS. ST. MAUGHAM*)* But I am not staying any longer! I want to go—

MRS. ST. MAUGHAM. *(Takes* LAUREL'S *hand)* —but you'll not take Laurel! I have a special knowledge of her! To me she is like a porcelain on a shelf—cracked in some marvellous way for the better!

OLIVIA. *(Turns to* JUDGE*)* My mother uses words in her special fashion! For a phrase—she would make capital of anything!

MRS. ST. MAUGHAM. Charming—for a mother to hear! And in front of an old friend! If—at a luncheon party— you want to have out the damage of a lifetime—

MADRIGAL. *(Loudly)* Let's have it!

MRS. ST. MAUGHAM. What?

MADRIGAL. I beg your pardon.

MRS. ST. MAUGHAM. Were you objecting?

MADRIGAL. *(Coming to front of sofa)* Yes. I think the wine has cut the caution.

(JUDGE *rises to behind sofa—gesturing.)*

MRS. ST. MAUGHAM. Don't gesture at me, Puppy!

JUDGE. Anything may precipitate—

MRS. ST. MAUGHAM. What?

MADRIGAL. Anything!

JUDGE. *(To* MADRIGAL*)* Will you come into another room—and I will advise you?

MADRIGAL. *(Turns to him)* No, Judge. Your advice is foreseen! That I must leave here— *(Steps up)* but it is the child who must leave! *(Turns)* Laurel must go, Mrs. St. Maugham, go with her mother.

(OLIVIA *moves up behind armchair.)*

MRS. ST. MAUGHAM. *(Rises)* You take a great liberty!

(LAUREL *moves down Left Centre.)*

MADRIGAL. Yes, now I have a sense of liberty.

MRS. ST. MAUGHAM. That is not what I meant!

MADRIGAL. No, but it is what I mean!

MRS. ST. MAUGHAM. This child of special soil!—Transplant her?

MADRIGAL. You have not a green thumb, Mrs. St. Maugham, with a plant or a girl. This is a house where nothing good can be made of her.

MRS. ST. MAUGHAM. *My* house!

MADRIGAL. *Your* house! Why even your garden is demented! By the mercy of God you do not keep an animal!

MRS. ST. MAUGHAM. You are mad! You are a monster!

MADRIGAL. No, I am a woman who has lost touch with things. With indulgence. With excuses, with making merry over bad things.

(MRS. ST. MAUGHAM *sits again.*)

The light—and the shade—has been hammered out of me. I am as humourless as a missionary.

JUDGE. Why complicate life? The past is over.

MADRIGAL. If the past is useful, I shall not hesitate to use it. What I have been has long been done with— *(To* LAUREL) What you are is yet to come. Let's *finish* with the charade made here of affection! . . .

MRS. ST. MAUGHAM. Stop the woman, Puppy! Stop her!

OLIVIA. But Miss Madrigal has something to say!

JUDGE. No, she hasn't.

MADRIGAL. Oh! I am not inexperienced! You must allow me a certain bias!

JUDGE. Have a care!

MADRIGAL. I am beyond caring!

LAUREL. *(Steps down stage—whispers)* Boss, Boss, don't go too far!

MADRIGAL. *(Crossing to above her)* Don't drive me to it! *(Taking her by the shoulders passionately)* Who else can tell you that when the moment comes when truth might serve you—you will not make it sound! Or that the clarion note—the innocence—will desert you! . . .

LAUREL. *(Crossing to Right Centre, faces Right)* But everybody *knows* about me! They know what happened!

MADRIGAL. They know what you have told them!

MRS. ST. MAUGHAM. Insolence!

MADRIGAL. You didn't stop the marriage, but you snatched the attention! Shall we now deprive your grandmother of your famous seduction?

(LAUREL *turns to face them.* JUDGE *sits in desk chair.*)

MRS. ST. MAUGHAM. At what a moment!

MADRIGAL. One has to *find* a moment to say such things.

OLIVIA. *(Left of chair—to* MADRIGAL*)* But is that what she said? *(To her mother)* Is that what you have believed?

MADRIGAL. Wait! *(Crosses to* LAUREL*)* Let the child tell you!

LAUREL. *(Backing away below sofa)* You were not there!

MADRIGAL. I did not need to be there. The story can be read backwards! *(Turns to* MRS. ST. MAUGHAM.*)* What newspaper did the cook take in, I wonder!

OLIVIA. A child of twelve!

MADRIGAL. An only child is never twelve! *(Turning to* LAUREL*)* Do you cry?

LAUREL. No.

MADRIGAL. *(Close to sofa)* I should cry.

LAUREL. I am not near crying.

MADRIGAL. *(Sits on sofa, takes her hand)* I should cry —with relief—that your mother wants you! *(Pause)* Be careful! Even a mother can't wait forever.

OLIVIA. *(Above armchair, to* MADRIGAL*)* But why did she pretend? Why did she make it up?

MADRIGAL. Odd things are done for love.

(LAUREL *runs to up Centre door, and stops—facing up stage.*)

OLIVIA. Give it up, Laurel! It isn't worth going on.

LAUREL. *(Comes down, to* MADRIGAL*)* Has it got to be the truth?

MADRIGAL. *(Half smiling)* One can lie— But truth is more interesting!

LAUREL. —and you get better and better at spotting it! You win, Boss!

(She turns and runs across down stage and upstairs. Pauses on the landing, then, when she sees OLIVIA *coming, disappears.)*

MADRIGAL. *(To* OLIVIA) Quick! A straw would break it. (OLIVIA *exits upstairs.)*
(She crosses to up Left calling softly after them) Your blue linen dress is folded in the top drawer. Look for your yellow striped one. *(Then moves slowly down Left and sits exhausted in lower chair.)*

(JUDGE *comes above sofa to* MRS. ST. MAUGHAM.)

MRS. ST. MAUGHAM. *(Gripping tooth and nail to the behaviour of a hostess as she lets fall the tin clatter of words. To the* JUDGE) *What* a precipitation—of melodrama—your visit's fallen on! *(Flame beginning to run in her tone)* Blood is thicker than water I had thought but it appears not!

JUDGE. *(Close to her)* My dear—my dear old friend—

MRS. ST. MAUGHAM. *(At height of passion. Rises)* If you were on your knees you wouldn't stop me! *(Turning to* MADRIGAL) *That* was a black patch, Miss Madrigal! If there's a fire to be lit—you've set a match to it! What collusion behind my back! *(To* JUDGE) You've been a witness to it!

JUDGE. You two would be better talking alone, I think. *(He starts to leave.)*

MRS. ST. MAUGHAM. Stay where you are, Puppy! Men are such cowards! *(Above chair)* In the name of discretion or a cool head or some such nonsense—they leave one in the lurch—

JUDGE. So much better—better not say anything!

MRS. ST. MAUGHAM. There's an undependability in

high-minded men! They sit—objective! When they should be burning beside one! But—when things become personal— *(To him)* What would you say if your clerk put your wig on!

JUDGE. *(Unhappily)* I should reflect at length, I expect, and decide on inaction.

MRS. ST. MAUGHAM. So you would! But I've been robbed of my grand-daughter!

MADRIGAL. *(Calmly)* If you face facts, Mrs. St. Maugham, you are tired of her.

MRS. ST. MAUGHAM. *(Faintly)* Be a man, Puppy! Put her out! Put her out in the street for me!

(The JUDGE *makes an unhappy movement of recoil.)* *(Turns to* MADRIGAL *with mounting passion)* The flaming impudence! The infamy! And I—lavish! Trusting—leaning— *(Crosses down to her)* But I've been leaning on a demon! In your heart—every penny should have scalded you! I've been betrayed. Don't talk to me of wages! You'll see none of them! *(Goes above, and round armchair.)*

JUDGE. *(Crossing to* MADRIGAL*)* Perhaps this is where I may be of some use?

MADRIGAL. *(Smiling gently)* No, Judge. Not now. Fifteen years ago you might have been.

MRS. ST. MAUGHAM. *(Front of sofa)* Do you dare to speak! What are these innuendos?

JUDGE. *(Low)* Least said, soonest mended. *(Sits upper chair down Left.)*

MRS. ST. MAUGHAM. Hints—since lunch—have been flying like gnats from side to side of the room. Nobody tells me—in plain English—anything! Have you two met before then?

MADRIGAL. *(Matter of fact)* I was once sentenced to death by the Judge here.

MRS. ST. MAUGHAM. Ah! *(Sinking into chair.)*

JUDGE. *(Rising)* Ill-advised. Ill-advised. *(To above Centre chair.)*

MRS. ST. MAUGHAM. *(Flying robustly up again)* Oh!

If I were not seventy this would revive me! To *death?*
—But *there you are!*

MADRIGAL. Those who still live—have to be some-where.

MRS. ST. MAUGHAM. If it's true—it's outrageous! And if I start putting two and three together— *Good heavens* —*how can you be living at all!*

JUDGE. There was a doubt.

MRS. ST. MAUGHAM. What I doubt is my senses! The thing's impossible! Either I don't believe it—or it's quite private! Besides, if it were true—it would be—most in-convenient! Oh—I would like the situation annulled! The conversation put back—

JUDGE. To where?

MRS. ST. MAUGHAM. To where it hadn't happened! *(Crossing to* MADRIGAL*)* And at the interview—how dared you—I let pass—so many excellent applicants in favour of you!

(JUDGE *to Right of Centre table.)*

MADRIGAL. *(Mildly)* No—really—it was not so.

MRS. ST. MAUGHAM. *(Struck by another thought)* —and the references! The references I had— I am amazed! You must have forged them!

MADRIGAL. I gave you none.

MRS. ST. MAUGHAM. Why?

MADRIGAL. *(Simply)* I had none.

JUDGE. *(Explaining mildly)* This lady came to you from prison.

MRS. ST. MAUGHAM. Prison! I would have thought a University. Oh, you have been most satisfactory, I *thought,* but now a light is thrown—I'm growing more and more thunder-struck!

MADRIGAL. But—

MRS. ST. MAUGHAM. Don't speak to me, if you please! *(Crossing Right)* You who come out of God-knows-what ancient Publicity! Blazing—from heaven-knows-what lurid newspapers! A headline! A felon! And how can you lunch with me, Puppy, and know such things! Oh I'm dumbfounded! *(Sits sofa, exhausted)* What's more, I've been defrauded! Go! Pack your bags! Pack your bags! Out of the house with you.

(MADRIGAL *rises. Enter* MAITLAND, *on a light wind of impatience. To above her.* JUDGE *turns to above sofa.)*

MAITLAND. I can't wait— I can't wait forever! *(To* MRS. ST. MAUGHAM, *who has practically collapsed)* Is she—who we think she is!

MRS. ST. MAUGHAM. *(In a faint groan)* She is.

MAITLAND. *(Turning radiantly to* MADRIGAL) Oh— Miss— Oh— Madam. (MAITLAND *bows slightly.)*

(MADRIGAL *gives a tiny bow in return.)*

MRS. ST. MAUGHAM. Heavens! What an anti-climax! What veneration! One would think the woman was an actress!

MAITLAND. When one is a humble man one can't express it. I think it is—to *think* that after such a gale she is with us.

MRS. ST. MAUGHAM. *(Feebly)* That's enough, Maitland.

MAITLAND. *(Turning)* To have stood one's life before the Judge here—if you'll pardon me, m'lord, even though you eat your lunch like other men—making the same light talk . . . *(Sharply as the down Right door opens)* Here's the Nurse! All of a dither!

NURSE. *(Rushing in)* Mrs. St. Maugham—

MRS. ST. MAUGHAM. *(In a daze)* We have friends now. It can wait, Nurse.

NURSE. *(Steps in behind sofa)* Mr. Pinkbell is dead.

MRS. ST. MAUGHAM. You can go, Nurse. I'll attend to it later.

(NURSE, *aghast, does not move.)*

I say *we have friends,* Nurse!

(NURSE *exits, horrified, leaving door open.*)

JUDGE. *(Above sofa)* But—good heavens—Pinkbell!

MRS. ST. MAUGHAM. *(Dazed)* He is in expert hands.

MAITLAND. *(Left of armchair)* But the poor old bastard. He has passed over!

MRS. ST. MAUGHAM. Is *that* what she said?

MAITLAND. They've downed him—stiff as a rod. He hasn't tomorrow— *(Struck by a worse thought)* He hasn't the rest of *today!*

MRS. ST. MAUGHAM. Dead—and my past goes with him—

JUDGE. *(Slowly down behind sofa)* Dear me, dear me. I am shocked. First to know he is alive. Then to learn that he isn't.

MRS. ST. MAUGHAM. *(Musing)* When I was a young woman he educated me—my manner with distinguished foreigners— He saw to my Ascots. He bought my wine in France for me. Is there an afterlife, Puppy?

JUDGE. I don't give judgments easily. But in this life you will miss him. *(He takes her hand.)*

MRS. ST. MAUGHAM. *(Not looking at him)* Alas, no. Shall you come again, Puppy? When the excitement of your week is over?

JUDGE. Too much happens in this house—for an old man. *(He releases her hand and returns above sofa.)*

MRS. ST. MAUGHAM. I am coming with you to your car. *(Rises)* Everyone—accusing everyone—has been tiring. *(Returns to her old manner)* Stay with her, Maitland, I shan't be long. Keep an eye on her. *(Crosses below* JUDGE *and above* MAITLAND—*exits by front door.)*

(MADRIGAL *sits in upper chair down Left.* JUDGE *signs to* MAITLAND *to get his cap and coat from hall, then comes above armchair to* MADRIGAL.)

JUDGE. After all, have you liked the life here?

MADRIGAL. *(With an ironic smile)* It has a hollow quality—which soothes me.

JUDGE. What shall you do?

MADRIGAL. I shall continue to explore—the *astonishment* of living!

JUDGE. *(Offering hand)* Goodbye, Miss Madrigal.

(She gives him her hand.)

(Rises) No man's infallible.

(JUDGE exits, taking cap and coat from MAITLAND in hall. MADRIGAL sits. MAITLAND returns to her.)

MAITLAND. *(In eager excitement)* Can I come where you're going? I will serve you. Together we could throw our five and fifteen years away from us! In the dustbin!

MADRIGAL. *(Smiling)* Not mine! *(Rises)* Not my fifteen years! *(Crosses below armchair for her things on up stage table)* I value them! They made me!

MAITLAND. *(Ecstatic he follows, Left of armchair, to her)* Ah—that's the strength I hanker after! That's what I've been missing! I was born to worship the stars! But I've never known *which* stars— *(Facing down stage he spreads his arms wide)* —when the whole heaven's full of them!

(MRS. ST. MAUGHAM returns.)

(On the same note:) I wish to give my notice!

MRS. ST. MAUGHAM. Again! You choose such odd moments! *(To table down Left.)*

MAITLAND. *(Coming Right of armchair)* I wish to accompany Miss Madrigal!

MRS. ST. MAUGHAM. Where to?

MAITLAND. Where she's going.

MRS. ST. MAUGHAM. *(Chooses a rose from vase on table)* Yet now you have it all your own way, Maitland.

MAITLAND. *(Wincing, glancing up at the ceiling)* Don't say that!

MRS. ST. MAUGHAM. *(Crossing below sofa)* I'll talk to you later— I must go up— *(As she exits, to herself)* —stiff as a rod—the poor old bastard— *(Leaves door open.)*

MADRIGAL. *(Turns from up stage table. Gardening*

book and apron under her arm, she refers to her note-
book) —thin out the seedlings—as I showed you—the
lilac wants pruning—and the rock-rose and the pasque
flower—

MAITLAND. *(Trying to interrupt)* But—

MADRIGAL. —tie in the black grape! Cut the heads on
the moss rose—

MAITLAND. But—

MADRIGAL. *(Turns to desk, taking no notice)* —the
asphodel and the dew plant—

MAITLAND. But what's to become of my decision!

MADRIGAL. *(In irritated despair that he doesn't listen)*
Oh—don't give notice so often! It's a fidgety habit! *(Sits
at desk.)*

(LAUREL and OLIVIA come downstairs. LAUREL now wears
a white linen dress, white straw hat and brown
leather sandals. She carries an overcoat and a suit-
case, which she leaves in the hall. She comes into the
room, below the armchair. OLIVIA remains on the
step.)

MAITLAND. *(Seeing her)* You look a proper daughter.

LAUREL. *(Going to him)* You may kiss me, Maitland.
(MAITLAND kisses her brow.)
(Turns to OLIVIA.) Maitland loves me.

OLIVIA. *(Comes into the room)* Loves you?

LAUREL. I had to have someone—*someone* who thought
the world of me.

OLIVIA. As I did?

LAUREL. *(Crosses to above her, takes her hand)* As you
do.

MRS. ST. MAUGHAM. *(Returns. Closes door)* Leave us,
Maitland!

(MAITLAND exits to pantry.)
(MRS. ST. MAUGHAM plays this scene magnificent and
relentless. Comes to front of sofa) You were right,
Olivia, when you said he and I had the same standards.

(Dry and gruff) Well, Laurel—now you have a mother! It's not so rare! Every kitten has one!

LAUREL. *(Steps forward—hands behind her)* Have you often seen death before, Grandloo—?

MRS. ST. MAUGHAM. Up till now I have managed to avoid it. *(Still rather sharp from several reasons—that she has been beaten in battle, also that MADRIGAL is in the room and she doesn't want LAUREL near her)* Don't begin badly! Where are your gloves?

LAUREL. *(On step forward—shows her gloves)* Grandloo—

MRS. ST. MAUGHAM. *(Her hand up to ward her off)* No goodbyes! I'm too old for them—

OLIVIA. Go to the car, darling. *(Pause)* Begin by obeying.

(LAUREL *crosses above* OLIVIA *on to second step. Turns and exchanges a look with* MADRIGAL, *who then turns back to desk.* LAUREL *takes her coat and suitcase and goes out.*)

MRS. ST. MAUGHAM. Well, Olivia? What are you going to do with her? Teach her the right things? After I've taught her the wrong ones?

OLIVIA. You're like an old Freethinker—who finds he has a son a clergyman.

MRS. ST. MAUGHAM. Is that so terrible?

OLIVIA. No— But to you inscrutable. *(One step forward)* *Why* did you want her?

MRS. ST. MAUGHAM. Is it a crime to want to be remembered?

(OLIVIA *turns away. Stops as she speaks.*)
The Pharoahs built the Pyramids for that reason.

OLIVIA. *(Turns, stung. Low)* Are the thoughts of a daughter . . . no sort of memorial?

MRS. ST. MAUGHAM. *(Unconquered)* Is that an obituary?

(OLIVIA *with a little defeated shake of her head goes out.*)

(Left alone Mrs. St. Maugham *runs to the window, Left, leans out, waiting for them to appear outside the front door. Calling through window robustly, the old Adam in her still in full sway)* Leave her hair long! It gives her the choice later! *(Pause. Louder)* Keep her bust high! *(She waits a moment.)*

(They are gone.)

(She turns, draws herself to her full height. Aridly, stoically) What do women do—in my case?

Madrigal. *(From the other side of the room)* They garden.

Mrs. St. Madrigal. But it seems I am not very good at that either. Are your things packed? *(Picks up garden catalogue.)*

Madrigal. *(Coldly)* I am a light-footed traveller.

Mrs. St. Maugham. *(Holding out the catalogue)* Before you go will you point out the white crinum? *(She hands it to her.)*

(Madrigal *takes it and looks at it.)*

You, who have an impertinent answer to everything—is there an afterlife? *(Sits in armchair—Centre stage.)*

Madrigal. Certainly.

Mrs. St. Maugham. *(Surprised)* You say—"certainly"?

Madrigal. *(Looking through catalogue)* One does not sit alone for fifteen years without coming to conclusions.

Mrs. St. Maugham. Is there—affection in it?

Madrigal. *(To Right of table)* But you have been living all this while without affection! Haven't you noticed it? *(She hands her the catalogue.)*

Mrs. St. Maugham. *(To this no answer. Puts her glasses on and reads aloud)* —"very rare—from the High Andes of Bolivia. Jasmine-like, tubular flowers. . . ."

Madrigal. Don't waste your time. They are beyond you.

Mrs. St. Maugham. *(Not raising her head)* It speaks wonderfully of the Uvularia.

Madrigal. When will you learn you live on chalk?

MRS. ST. MAUGHAM. *(On same tone)* I have made such a muddle of the heart. Will Olivia forgive me?

MADRIGAL. It is pointless to wonder. You have no choice how she will sum up. *(Pause. Quietly)* She will live longer.

MRS. ST. MAUGHAM. *(Vexed)* Am I to die unloved?

MADRIGAL. If necessary. *I* was prepared to do it.

MRS. ST. MAUGHAM. *(Looking front)* The Unicorn Root—

MADRIGAL. *(Looks towards garden—then moves down Right)* —needs a sheltered spot. You haven't one.

MRS. ST. MAUGHAM. *(Slowly)* If you stay here—you can grow windbreaks— *(Suddenly, turning and taking her glasses off)* I must know one thing!

MADRIGAL. What?

MRS. ST. MAUGHAM. *(Her face agleam with human curiosity, she looks at* MADRIGAL*)* Did you do it?

MADRIGAL. *(Unperturbed and calm)* What learned men at the top of their profession couldn't find out in nine days—why should you know?

MRS. ST. MAUGHAM. *(Looking down at the catalogue and putting her glasses on, after a second's pause)* —the Dierama—the Wand Flower—

MADRIGAL. Won't grow on chalk. *(Crosses to her. With a strange still certainty that sits like a nimbus on her)* But if I stay with you—and we work together—with potash —and a little granular peat— We can *make* it do so.

(They look at each other.)

CURTAIN

END OF PLAY

THE CHALK GARDEN

FURNITURE

(Set Dressing and Property Setup)

ACT ONE

(Note: * = Working Properties)

D.L. window
1 pair of print drapes and valance
Practical traveller track
Green metal bird cage (hanging in window)
*White wooden, open armchair with seat pad (back
    against window)
    On D.L. wall
Antique woodmen barometer
    Below D.L. flat
*Round wooden 34" pedestal table— 2'4" high
    On table
Green cloth covering
*Can of nicotine for garden
*Black coffee tin with lace handkerchief inside
*1 pair of garden gloves
*White flowered bowl filled with sand
Small blue vase with cornflowers
Small standing oval picture frame with picture
Small, brown modern vase with a red and white lily
Large, scalloped, yellow glass vase with red and white
    dahlias
Small, pink and gold vase with dahlias, carnations and
    little pink flowers

Small, light-blue vase with dahlias
White china tray
Three garden catalogues
On tray: Green gold-trimmed flowered cup; small gold
yellow and white cup
S.R. of table
*White wooden open armchair with seat pad
*3 blue upholstered side chairs
S.L. hall door flat
2 oval, gold framed pictures on either side of door
Plaster of paris face C. of cornice above door
U.S.L.
*Black lacquer Chinese sideboard with marble top—3'6"
long, 1'6" wide, 3'5½" high
On sideboard:
Green tin box U.C.
Brown Mexican bowl L.C.
Green leaf cup R.C.
Large brown pitcher with Love-lies-bleeding U.L.
Tall vaseline vase with foxglove U.R.
Shelf 1 (top—S.L.) 3 books
Shelf 2 (bottom—S.L.) 4 books, *butler's tray and brush
Shelf 3 (top—S.R.) 6 books
Shelf 4 (bottom—S.R.) yellow roses in glass vase—small
brown book
U.C. shelves
Top Shelf (S.L. to S.R.) *3 copies of *The Notable Trial*
series; *1 large petal vase; *1 small petal vase;
large green vase with large yellow and white lilies;
*brown pitcher
Middle shelf: Books; yellow pitcher
Bottom shelf: Books
U.C.
*Print chaise—4'9" x 3'6" x 1'5" high
On chaise: 4 pillows (head of chaise); *long, shallow
wicker basket (D.S.)
R. of arch
Against wall: Long wooden handle; long garden fork;
3-pronged hoe; white, low, highbacked wooden chair

R. of chair
*Garden table—7'0" x 1'10" x 2'8" high
    On table (S.L. to S.R.):
5 assorted straw garden hats
Large wicker covered jug with "love-lies-bleeding"
Large pottery ice water cooler
Round shallow wicker basket with straw hat in it
Brown feather duster
Large art book (with spray can, 3-in-1 oil can, small
      weeder, 2 bunches of garlic, and small rag on it)
Large oblong basket with red straw hat in it
2 shallow oblong wicker baskets and a large coolie hat on
     top
Wooden brass-bound box with a 4-drawer, metal cabinet
     on it
Garden shears in front of box
    Shelf under table:
Large wicker basket with cover
Muddy galoshes
Wicker basket on side with raffia falling from it
Brown wicker basket with handle
Large round basket
Pair of raffia slippers
Large oblong basket with handle
    S.L. of garden table
*Small drop-leaf table, 2'4" round when opened, 2'1" high
    Hanging on L. garden window
String of garlic
Bunch of oregano
    Hanging on wall—R. of garden window
Small carpet beater
Limb saw
    Leaning against wall
Hoe
Scraper
Shovel
    On wall D.S. of Pinkbell door (facing D.S.)
*House phone with bell

Shelf niche in D.R. wall

Niche flanked by 2 porcelain urns

    Shelf 1 (top): Small pink vase—small gold and green cup

    Shelf 2: 3 painted leaf plates standing on brackets

    Shelf 3: 3 painted leaf plates standing on brackets

    Shelf 4: Books

    *Red lacquer slant-top desk (below niche)—3'8" x 1'6" (closed) x 3' high

    On top of desk: (D.S. to U.S.)

Tall green glass vase with thistle

Small white cup

Small brown, white-striped vase with 4 white flowers

Tiny white and gold vase

Marble bird

Tiny apple

Painted leaf plate on bracket

Brass match holder

Medium apple

Small brown, white striped vase with 5 white flowers

Big apple

Green glass candlestick

Matching marble bird

Chianti bottle with syringa

    On open leaf of desk (D.S. to U.S.)

For pigeon holes: books, pads, letters, catalogues, etc.

Large brown and white bowl with dahlias

*Garden catalogues

*Letters

Biggest apple

*Address book

Glass paper weight

*Glasses in case (Mrs. St. Maugham's)

Pencils

Gold trimmed picture cup

    Onstage of desk

*White wooden open armchair with seat pad

    Downstage of desk

Parasol

*Small upholstered armchair (chintz matching chaise)
    2'2" x 2'4"—seat: 1'3" high—back: 2'8" high
    Stage R.C.
*Large tan Victorian armchair (3'6" x 2'8", seat; 1'6",
    high-back; 3'0" high
 Chintz covered (matching chaise) pillow on chair
    Each side of chair
*2 (each side) small pie shaped wooden tables (1'5½" x
    1'5½")
    On table #1 (U.L. of chair)
 Varicolored glass vase with tall iris and thistle
 Small barble vase with purple and yellow conrflowers
 Small brown pot with purple and yellow cornflowers
 Bud vase with two large carnations
 White vase with different carnations
    On table #2 (D. L. of chair)
 Petal bowl with red and white lilies
    On table #3 (U.R. of chair)
 Glass horn vase on base with four yellow and one white
    carnations
*Small silver handbell
 Small Mexican ceramic holder with cornflowers
 Small glass vase with large carnation and tiny white
    flowers
    On table #4 (D.R. of chair)
 Small glass fishbowl with 2 gardenias
 Shell vase with cornflowers
 Gold trimmed cap with Sweet William
    On floor at D.R. leg of chair
*Small wicker basket
 In basket: 2 pads; lace handkerchief
    S.L. hall backing
 In wall niche—6 assorted pieces of broken china
 Under wall niche—black lacquer Chinese cabinet
    *Pre-set offstage Right for Act One (*all practical)*
 Book
 Large barrel-shaped garden basket on wheels
 Long handled shears in basket
 Raffia hanging over handle of basket

Garden trug across top of basket
In trug: Sweet William; daisies; small garden tools
Small watering can
4 long white and yellow lilies
 Pre-set offstage L. for Act One (*all practical)
Letter
Small tray
On tray: Bottle of Bols Creme de-Menthe; 2 liqueur
 glasses

ACT TWO

Strike
On D.L. table: Everything, including cloth cover
On sideboard: Everything on top
Garden trug on chair R. of arch
Chaise
On desk: Clear open leaf (make room for coffee tray)
On small table U.R. of armchair: Everything but horn
 vase on base; strike flowers from horn vase
On small table U.L. of armchair: Everything but differ-
 ent colored carnations
On small table D.R. of armchair: Everything
On desk: Bowl of flowers
On garden table: Wicker covered jug with "Love-lies-
 bleeding"
On U.C. shelves: Lilies from green vase
 Place
Pedestal table to R.C. marks
On table:
 *2 place mats (D.L. and D.R.) set with knife, fork
  and spoon, the spoons inside the knives
 Small bowl of "Sweet William" in Center of table
 *2 place mats U.R.
 *Chamois with 2 forks, 2 spoons, 2 knives—R.C.
Small drop leaf table to D.L. marks
On table:
 *Paint block and pencil
 *Small vase with one flower

*Glass half filled with water, with water color brushes
in it
*Palette (for water colors) with paint already in it
*Grey chaise (4'2" x 2', seat 1'8" high) to R.C. marks
 Print and tan pillows on chaise
*Large tan armchair to L.C. marks
*3 small tables around armchair
*1 small table next to U.L. corner of chaise
*Small side table in D.L. window covered with green cloth
        from pedestal table Act One
 Magazine rack with garden catalogues against D.L. wall
*White open wooden armchair S.L. of drop leaf table
 On chair:
        *Old mahogany paint box with lid open
         In box: Assorted tubes of water color paint
         Rag.
*White open wooden armchair S.R. of sideboard
*Small upholstered armchair U.S. of drop leaf table
 On small table U.L. of armchair:
        Glass horn vase (from U.R. table Act One), two
            white roses in vase
        White pitcher with maroon hollihocks
        White small vase with carnations
 On small table S.R. of armchair:
        Shaving mug with carnations (red, pink and white)
        Gold and pink vase with roses
        Green vase with carnations
 On garden table:
        Tall clear glass vase with 3 roses (pink)
 On desk: Large blue vase with rosebuds and assorted car-
        nations
 On U.C. shelves: In garden vase: White tobacco flowers
 On sideboard, which is a consol table converted to this
        use:
        White china fruit bowl with wax fruit
        Small silver toothpick holder with toothpicks
 Offstage R. (*all practical)
        Basket with quart bottle, funnel, small garden tools
            large measuring cup

Offstage L. (*all practical)
> Large serving tray
>> On tray: 4 dinner plates, napkins, wine glasses
>>> Small silver tray: 2 salt cellars, 2 pepper shakers, 1 pepper mill, 1 mustard pot
>> Small turpentine bottle
>> Rag
> *Bottle of Chablis with cork, opener, and napkin
> *Medium tray: *Sherry decanter, Sherry bottle, *3 sherry glasses
> *Round silver tray: *Silver coffee pot; *4 demitasse cups, saucers, and spoons
> *Large platter: *Sliced and quartered chicken; *mint leaves, aspic, etc., *serving fork and spoon
> *Wooden salad bowl with lettuce salad and wooden servers
> 3 chamois skins
> *Assorted rags
> *Long-stemmed pink lilies
> *Tall blue glass vase
> *2 glasses (1 breakaway)

ACT THREE

Strike

All luncheon dishes, food, etc., from tables; plates, silver, salt and pepper, mustard, napkins, mats, "Sweet William" from Center table, etc.

From sideboard: Serving tray, salad bowl, china fruit stand, toothpick holder

Side table in D.L. window: Paint box, flower, brushes, glass, palette on table

Drawing pad on U.C. shelves

On garden table: Basket, with funnel, measuring cup, quart bottle and tools

On small table L. of grey chaise—tray with sherry

On small chair R. of C. arch—trug

Place

Drop leaf table back to Act One position U.R. corner at
     end of garden table
Pedestal table to Act One marks, D.L.
On it:
> Green cover
> Large painted white pedestal vase with Lupin
> Small black and white bud vase with 3 rubber leaves
> Photograph album
> On it: *Catalogue
> *Coffee tray with cups, saucers, spoons
> *Two other catalogues
> *Mrs. St. Maugham's glasses case

*2 white open wooden chairs to Act Three marks near
     pedestal table D.L.; 1 U.R. by table; the other D.L.
     of table
*Tan armchair to C. Act Three marks
*4 small tables around armchair
 Flowers on upstage small tables remain as in Act Two
 D.S. small tables empty
*Grey chaise D.S. to Act Three marks—R. of tan armchair
 Small upholstered chair to D.R. below desk
 Open wooden white armchair to above desk under house
     phone
On sideboard:
> Large brass urn with lilies and green leaves
> *Gardening notebook (small)
> Green tin box, brown Mexican bowl, green leaf cup
>   as in Act One
*Mrs. St. Maugham's glasses—hang on D.R. bracket on
     wall above desk

THE CHALK GARDEN

ELECTRICAL FOCUS AND PLUG-IN PLOT

(For focusing, except where otherwise indicated, the furniture is placed for opening of Act One.)

BALCONY

#	S.W.	Aux.	Type	Watt	Color	Focus
1	1	-	LEKO	500	29	S.L.
2	2	-	"	"	54	S.L.
3	3	-	"	"	2/54	S.L.
4	1	-	"	"	2	S.L. lunch table Act Two
5	2	-	"	"	2	S.R.C.
6	3	-	"	"	2/54	S.R.C.
7	1	-	"	"	29	S.R.C.
8	2	-	"	"	2	C.
9	3	-	"	"	2/54	C.
10	1	-	"	"	29	L.C.
11	2	-	"	"	2	L. of C.
12	3	-	"	"	2/54	L. of C.
13	1	-	"	"	29	S.R.
14	2	-	"	"	54	L.C.
15	3	-	"	"	2/54	L.C.
16	1	-	"	"	2	S.R. lunch table Act Two
17	2	-	"	"	2	S.R.
18	3	-	"	"	2/54	S.R.C.

1st PIPE

#	S.W.	Aux.	Type	Watt	Color	Focus
1	6	29	LEKO	500	54	D.S.L. wall. Frame to light streak painted on wall

#	S.W.	Aux.	Type	Watt	Color	Focus
2	6	30	"	"	2/54	Front of sideboard. L. of hall door
3	6	31	FRES	"	2/54	U.S.L.
4	6	32	"	"	2/54	Chaise
5	6	33	"	"	2/54	U.L.C.
6	7	-	LEKO	"	62	Pinkbell door—Cut into door
7	6	34	"	"	3	Act Three position of armchair (cover Mrs. St. M. & Madrigal at end of show)
8	7	-	FRES	"	2/54	S.R. of onstage applicant chair
9	7	-	"	"	2/54	U. of D.L. table
10	7	-	"	"	2/54	Armchair
11	7	-	"	"	2/54	S.R. of armchair
12	8	41	LEKO	"	62	U.C.—keep off arch
13	7	-	"	"	62	Hall door—cut into door
14	8	42	FRES	"	2/54	Front of sideboard
15	8	43	"	"	2/54	S.L. applicant chair
16	8	44	"	"	2/54	U.S.L.
17	8	45	"	"	2/54	Front of S.L. garden window
18	8	46	LEKO	"	3	Act Three position of armchair (cover Mrs. St. M. & Madrigal at end of show)
19	9	-	FRES	"	2/54	U.L. of armchair
20	9	-	"	"	2/54	Armchair
21	9	-	"	"	2/54	U.S. of armchair

#	S.W.	Aux.	Type	Watt	Color	Focus
22	9	-	"	"	2/54	Below C. garden window
23	9	-	"	"	2/54	Desk chair
24	9	-	LEKO	"	2/54	S.L. applicant chair

2nd PIPE

#	S.W.	Aux.	Type	Watt	Color	Focus
1	10	53	FRES	500	2/54	D.S.C.
2	10	54	"	"	"	D.S.R.C.
3	10	55	"	"	"	D.S.R.
4	10	56	"	"	"	U.L. R. of hall door
5	10	57	"	"	(2/54 (Hi-Hat	U.C. Keep off arch
6	10	58	"	"	2/54	Below S.R. arch column
7	11	59	"	"	"	S.R. area L. of wall niche
8	11	60	"	"	"	D.S.L.C.
9	11	61	"	"	"	D.C.
10	11	62	"	"	"	D.S.R.C.

BEAM

#	S.W.	Aux.	Type	Watt	Color	Focus
1	26	65	FRES	500	(2/54 (Hi-Hat	U.C. below arch
2	26	66	"	"	1/17	S.L. wall toning
3	26	67	"	"	1/17	L.C. wall toning
4	26	68	"	"	62	U.L.
5	26	69	"	"	(2/54 (Hi-Hat	Maitland door
6	26	70	"	"	1/17	R.C. wall toning
7	11	59	"	"	1/17	S.R. wall toning
8	27	72	"	"	2/54	U.C. below arch

S.R. TORMENTOR

#	S.W.	Aux.	Type	Watt	Color	Focus
1	12	35	LEKO	500	2/54	D.S.L.
2	12	36	"	"	"	D.S.L.C.
3	12	37	"	"	"	D.S.C.
4	12	38	"	"	"	D.S.R.C.

#	S.W.	Aux.	Type	Watt	Color	Focus
5	12	39	"	"	"	D.S.R.
6	12	40	FRES	"	"	Desk chair

S.L. TORMENTOR

#	S.W.	Aux.	Type	Watt	Color	Focus
1	13	47	LEKO	500	2/54	D.S.R.
2	13	48	"	"	"	D.S.R.C.
3	13	49	"	"	"	D.S.C.
4	13	50	"	"	"	D.S.L.C.
5	13	51	"	"	"	D.S.L.
6	13	52	FRES	"	(2/54 (Hi-Hat	S.L. applicant chair & below D.C. table

FOOTLIGHTS

#	S.W.	Aux.	Type	Watt	Color	Focus
4				75/75	62	Keep off ceiling
5				"	3	Keep off ceiling
14				"	29	Keep off ceiling

ARCH

#	S.W.	Aux.	Type	Watt	Color	Focus
1	15	-	FRES	500	2/54	Garden door
2	15	-	"	"	1/17	Wash U.S. stone wall

OFFSTAGE L. D.S.

#	S.W.	Aux.	Type	Watt	Color	Focus
1(U.S.)	21		LEKO	1500	54/54	Through D.L. window
2(c)	28		FRES	1000	54/54	Wash stone wall backing & D.L. window
3(D.S.)	28		LEKO	1500	54/54	Thru bottom of window & D.S. L. wall

S.L. HALL BOOM

#	S.W.	Aux.	Type	Watt	Color	Focus
1	28	64	LEKO	500	2/54	Thru hall door
2	28	63	FRES	500	2/54	Backing & niche
1	27	75	WIZ	250	69	Entrance

BUTLER'S HALL

#	S.W.	Aux.	Type	Watt	Color	Focus
1	27	76	FRES	500	2/54	Off wall—for en- trance

U.S.L. GARDEN BOOM

#	S.W.	Aux.	Type	Watt	Color	Focus
1	25		LEKO	500		Garden entrance
1	27	73	WIZ	250	69	Pinkbell door—offstage

U.S.R. GARDEN BOOM (D.S.)

| 1 | 25 | | LEKO | 500 | 54/54 | Thru transom & garden door |
| 2 | 25 | | LEKO | 500 | 54/54 | Thru garden door —off posts |

U.S.R. GARDEN BOOM (U.S.)

| 1 | 23 | | FRES | 1500 | 54/54 | Thru top of garden window |
| 2 | 23 | | FRES | 1500 | 54/54 | Flood bottom of garden window |

GARDEN WINDOW XRAY

| | 24 | | R-40 | | 30/30 | 15 light 3 circuit |
| | 27 | 75 | FRES | 100 | White | Thru transom above garden door |

U.S. OF GARDEN WALL (On Floor)

1	22		FRES	100	29	Straight up— streak drop
2	22		"	"	29	Straight up— streak drop
3	22		"	"	2/2	Straight up— streak drop
4	22		"	"	29	Straight up— streak drop

#3 PIPE—2 Sections, 15 light, 3 circuit

16	$-40	150	54
16	R-40	150	3
17	R-40	150	43

#4 PIPE—2 Sections, 15 light, 3 circuit

18	R-40	150	54
18	R-40	150	3
			4-3's

#	S.W.	Aux.	Type	Watt	Color	Focus
	19		R-40	150	White	

#5 PIPE—2 Sections, 15 light, 3 circuit

#	S.W.	Aux.	Type	Watt	Color	Focus
	20		R-40	150	White	
	20		R-40	150	White	

MISCELLANEOUS

#	S.W.	Aux.	Type
	27	74	**FAN**

U.L. Level with garden wall
—focussed on Borders
S.L. Hall—Phone bell
S.L. Hall—Door buzzer
On S.R. wall—House phone
Signal light outside D.L. window

THE CHALK GARDEN

WARDROBE

MRS. ST. MAUGHAM
Act One
Beige dress-jacket
Rope of pearls, scarf, pair of brown brogues
Beige linen shoes, garden hat (straw), beige gloves
Act Two
Pink dress—jacket—stockings
2 straw hats (tan)
Garden apron (beige)
Pair tennis shoes (beige)
Grey kid shoes
Glasses
1 pink scarf
2 pearl bracelets—earrings
5 strand pearl necklace, rings—pearls, diamonds
Clip (rhinestones) holding small green leaf

MADRIGAL
Act One
Grey suit—blouse (white)
Pair brown kid gloves
Bag—brown leather
Locket—chain
Stockings—hat (straw sailor)—brown shoes
Act Two
Lavender dress with jacket
Canvas apron—gloves—hair piece
Pair garden shoes
Pair grey shoes (suede)

Olivia
Act One
Raw silk beige dress—coat—hat (brown net cloche)
Scarf—gloves—shoes (black)
Hair piece
Act Three
Green surplice dress with jacket
Green hat
Jewelry—2 bracelets
String of pearls
Light green scarf
Black suede shoes

2ND Applicant
Green silk dress
Plaid cape (wool)
Hat—bag—gloves—jewelry (beads)—black shoes

3RD Applicant
Lavender suit—hat to match color of suit
Beaded bag—lace front grey shoes—gloves—jewelry
(necklace of beads)
Lace front blouse

Nurse
Blue striped uniform
White collar—cuffs—belt
White stockings—white shoes—headdress

Maitland
Butler's white jacket
3 ties (2 black—1 stripe)
Striped trousers
White shirt
Black shoes, black socks
Gold framed glasses

Laurel
Act One
White duck pants
Blue blouse

Wig—jewelry—(2 necklaces) rhinestones
Act Two
White sailor blouse
Yellow skirt
Pink sandals
Act Three
Same as Act Two
Grey tweed coat
Grey beret
White gloves
White nylon slip

JUDGE
Wool vest (beige)
Grey tweed overcoat
Handkerchief (breast pocket)
Dark glasses
Brown tweed suit
Brown shoes
White shirt
Brown socks
Dark blue figured tie

THE CHALK GARDEN

PRESS REPORTS

"On Wednesday night a wonder happened: The West End Theatre justified its existence. . . . One had thought it an anachronism, wilfully preserving a formal, patrician acting style for which the modern drama has no use, a style as remote from reality as a troop of cavalry in an age of turbo-jets. One was shamefully wrong. On Wednesday night, superbly caparisoned, the cavalry went into action and gave a display of theatrical equitation which silenced all grumblers. . . . The occasion of its triumph was Enid Bagnold's *The Chalk Garden* (Haymarket) which may well be the finest artificial comedy to have flowed from an Egnlish (as opposed to an Irish) pen since the death of Congreve. . . . We eavesdrop on a group of thoroughbred minds, expressing themselves in speech of an exquisite candour, building ornamental bridges of metaphor, tiptoeing across frail causeways of simile, and vaulting over gorges impassable to the rational soul."—Kenneth Tynan, *The Observer* (London)

"*The Chalk Garden* is an English rose of comedy."—Philip Hope-Wallace, *Manchester Guardian*

"Triumph! For a play nobody wanted."—*Daily Express* (London)

"Further, we know that one of the chief productions of this New York season is Miss Enid Bagnold's *The Chalk Garden*. We watched for the appearance of the play as eagerly as any ship-wrecked mariner ever scanned the horizon for the sight of a rescuing sail. . . . The atmosphere at the Haymarket Theatre last Wednesday was therefore electric. . . . At the end the applause was tremendous. There were such shouts for the author as I have not heard in a London Theatre for several years. No word less strong than triumphant will serve for the reception the audience gave to *The Chalk Garden*. . . . These are facts. It is also a fact that I did not like *The Chalk Garden*."—Harold Hobson, *(The Sunday Times* (London)

"Magic, by gum!"—*Daily Herald* (London)

'But, bless it, this isn't a play that needs stars—it *deserves them*."—M.D.V., *Evening Argus* (Brighton, England)

"I realised that Miss Bagnold's dialogue was likely to withstand—as some West End triumphs fail to do—the merciless, exacting usuage of the years. There is a quality of permanence here. . . . One of the prime virtues of *The Chalk Garden* is that it is theatrical as well as literary."—J. C. Trewin, *Illustrated London News*

"I am afraid I don't like this kind of thing. . . . Is it art? Is it entertainment? . . ."—Anthony Hartley, *Spectator*

"*The Chalk Garden* is a coruscating piece of work— witty in the literary tradition of Congreve. . . . There is a stimulating mind at work in *The Chalk Garden*. It is courageous, subtle and detached. It is one of the keenest minds that have upset the complacence of Broadway for a long time."—Brooks Atkinson, *New York Times*

"Whatever is being communicated is communicated eliptically around psychological corners, with the impulsiveness of thundergolts out of clear blue skies . . . a vision of what a very fresh and personal kind of play could be like, and she has seen it through with wit, literacy, and an almost unearthly integrity."—Walter F. Kerr, *New York Herald Tribune*

"Once in a very great while a new play comes along that lives in the intangibles of heart and human will: a play that is extremely poetic without the formalising rhythm of verse, that is witty without the exaggeration of farce. Such a play is *The Chalk Garden*."—*Saturday Review of Literature*

"Playwright Bagnold's sidelong, elegantly savage play . . ."—*Time*

"New York has been favored by being allowed to see Enid Bagnold's *The Chalk Garden* before London."— *Christian Science Monitor*

The Award of Merit Medal of the American Academy of Arts and Letters, together with $1,000 for Distinguished Achievement in the Arts of the Drama, has been awarded to Enid Bagnold, "as a highly outstanding person in America" and was presented by Maxwell Anderson, President of the Academy, on May 23rd 1956.

OUR TOWN

Drama. 3 acts. By Thornton Wilder. 17 males, 7 females, extras. Bare stage. Costumes, 1901.

Winner of the Pulitzer Prize, 1939. The play begins in 1901 in Grover's Corners where the Gibbs and the Webbs are neighbors. During their childhood George Gibbs and Emily Webb are playmates and their lives are inextricably woven together as neighbor's lives are like to be. But as they grow older they pass from this period into a state of romantic but embarrassed interest in one another. And one day, after a slight quarrel, George proposes to Emily in the drug store over an ice cream soda. They are a fine young couple, but their happiness is short-lived, for Emily is taken in death and placed in the village cemetery on a rainy, dreary day. In the most vitally moving scene in the modern theatre is shown the peace and quiet of death which can never be understood by the living. Emily, at first, doesn't understand it, and not until she has gone back to relive her twelfth birthday does she understand that life is a transient fleeting thing and death brings an eternal peace. She takes her place in the graveyard with her friends while George, unable to see beyond his grief, mourns for her.

(Royalty, $25.00.)

TEN LITTLE INDIANS

Mystery. 3 acts. By Agatha Christie. 9 males, 3 females. Interior. Modern costumes.

A superlative type of mystery comedy, first produced at the Broadhurst Theatre in New York. The play takes place in a weird old house on an island. In the house is a mantel-piece on which there are ten little wooden Indians, and above which is an inscription of the nursery rhyme, telling how each little Indian died—until there were none. Ten people are gathered in the house as guests of a mysterious and unseen host. They hear the voice of the host accuse them, each in his turn, of complicity in a murder. Then one by one the guests suffer the different deaths predicted by the voice, and one by one the little wooden Indians topple. With seven down and three to go, the audience is still suspicious and in a fever of excitement. What follows is a tremendously gripping finale, expertly done by one America's top mystery writers.

(Royalty, $50.00.)

LO AND BEHOLD

Comedy. 3 acts. By John Patrick.

5 men, 3 women. Interior. Modern costumes.

This comedy has to do with a Nobel Prize Winner who has lived for many years on a meagre, unpalatable diet, to favor an ailing heart. This very lack of much heart has made the philosophy of his books coldly cynical. After signing a will that leaves a third of his estate to his young doctor, a third to perpetuate his house as a sanctuary for his spirit, and the final third to the Harvard Law School to insure that the terms of his odd testament will be carried out, he eats a sumptuous meal and dies happily. Instead of the solitude he has expected to find, he is beset by the spirits of an Indian girl pushed off a cliff by her lover, a Southern belle with a disturbing drawl and a phony liberal attitude, and a frustrated composer. As if this weren't enough to annoy the soul of an aesthete, the pretty cook (a former model) who had prepared the fatal dishes, returns to the house and is mistaken for his daughter. The author eventually finds peace in furthering a romance between the doctor and the young girl. Another surefire hit for those High Schools and Little Theatres that enjoyed *The Hasty Heart* and *The Curious Savage*, by the same author. "Its idea is amusing and so are the players, and Patrick has learned the trick of inserting a big, solid laugh line at the right moment."—*Daily News.*
(Royalty, $50-$25.)

LACE ON HER PETTICOAT

Drama. 3 acts. By Aimee Stuart.

2 men, 5 women. Interior. 1890 English costumes.

In her play, the author is telling the story of two little girls, on an island off the west coast of Scotland in 1890, who take a great fancy to one another. One is the daughter of a young widow who owns a shop in Glasgow, and the other is the child of the local peer, and, even though the children have developed a genuine mutual fondness, mother and grandmother of the poor girl are sure that nothing good will come of it. For a time it seems that their suspicions are unjustified, but, finally, class lines are drawn, and the hearts of the two little girls are broken. "A gentle and tearful little Scottish drama. . . . Both charming and touching."—*N. Y. Post.* "It has grace and form."—*N. Y. Times.* "Particularly poignant."—*Daily Mirror.* A splendid vehicle for High Schools, Colleges, and Community Theatres.
(Royalty, $25-$20.)

ANTIGONE
Tragedy, no act division. Translated by
Lewis Galantiere from the French of Jean Anouilh.
8 males, 4 females. Interior. Modern costumes.

Produced in modern dress—white ties and evening gowns
—at the Cort Theatre in New York with Katharine Cornell
as Antigone and Sir Cedric Hardwicke as Creon. The two
sons of Oedipus, late King of the ancient Greek city of
Thebes, had started a civil war and both were killed. Their
uncle Creon became Regent. This version of the ancient
Greek legend comes from a Paris that was suffering under
the heel of Nazi tyranny. The play's parallels to modern
times are easily grasped, are exciting and provocative.
Creon, resembling in thought and action a latter day Totali-
tarian, ordains that one of the brothers who had in his
opinion provoked the civil war be left unburied—carrion
for dogs and vultures. Antigone, an individualist clinging to
a higher law, covers the body of her brother with earth
Creon has her buried alive for punishment, which act brings
about the death of his son, who was in love with Antigone,
provokes his wife into taking her own life, and eventually
brings about his own ruin. "The first really thought-pro-
voking play to come along for some time."—*New York Post*
(Royalty, $25-$20.)

MEDEA
Play. 2 acts. By Robinson Jeffers.
Freely adapted from the Medea of Euripides.
5 males, 5 females (extras). Exterior. Greek costumes.

Opened at the National Theatre in New York to the
unanimous acclaim of the critics, who agreed that this is a
play for actual performance in the theatre as well as for
the contemplation and enjoyment of the discerning reader
This, his most eloquent drama, reaffirms Jeffers' preem-
inent place among modern poets. In this version of the
Greek Classic, the ambitious Jason forsakes Medea, his
foreign wife, and takes a new bride for political advance-
ment. Now alone in a strange land, Medea rages with
thoughts of revenge. On the day of her banishment she
succeeds in bringing death to the new young bride and the
most wanton horror to her husband, Jason. "Euripides'
tragedy, *Medea*, with fine new words by Robinson Jeffers,
and the works, in the way of acting, by Judith Anderson
won cheers and thirteen curtain calls last night at the
National Theatre."—*N. Y. Daily News.*
(Royalty, $50-$25.)

BLITHE SPIRIT

Farce. 3 acts. By Noel Coward. 2 males, 5 females. Interior. Modern costumes.

The smash comedy hit of the London and Broadway stages. The ingenious plot tells how novelist Charles Condomine invites to his country home an eccentric lady medium in order to learn the language of the occult. Neither Charles nor his second wife has any idea that the seance by the medium could summon back Charles' first wife from the beyond. But in she comes, a jealous and mischievous spirit, to torment Charles and break up his marriage. Soon we realize that the first wife is planning a fatal automobile accident for Charles, so that he might join her in a tryst beyond the grave. The scheme misfires and, instead of Charles, the second wife is killed in the accident and passes over to the beyond. There are now two feminine and very blithe spirits, and the trouble they cause Charles provides a ringing climax to a corking good farce. "Hilariously funny, brilliant, clever, and about as cockeyed as a play can be and still stay on the stage."—*N. Y. Journal-American.*

(Royalty, $50.00.)

PARLOR STORY

Comedy. 3 acts. By William McCleery. 6 males, 4 females. Interior. Modern costumes.

This witty and provocative comedy was produced in New York at the Biltmore Theatre. Charles Burnett is a militantly liberal college professor who wants very much to be president of the university. He spurns offers of $20,000 and up as managing editor of a newspaper to teach journalism. His wife is a scheming go-getter who stages his campaign. The office of president is a political appointment, and the governor wants to use it to win votes in the impending election. The upshot of it is that the badgered professor finds his parlor cluttered up with State Troopers, a press tycoon and the Governor. A checker-like game of give and take and double cross ensues. To better his chances for the big college job, the professor is called upon to expel a student, in love with his daughter, for writing a muddled, daring editorial for the campus paper. He refuses, and through a chain of events becomes a strong man, a fighting man, a champion of liberalism in politics. "Some of the most beguiling dialogue of the season."—*N. Y. Times.*

(Royalty, $35.00.)

WITNESS FOR THE PROSECUTION

Melodrama. 3 acts. By Agatha Christie

17 men, 5 women. Interior. Modern costumes.

Winner of New York Critics Circle Award and the Antoinette Perry Award. One of the greatest mystery melodramas in years. The story is that of a likable young drifter who is suspected of bashing in the head of a middle-aged, wealthy spinster who has willed her tidy estate to him. His only alibi is the word of his wife, a queer customer, indeed, who, in the dock, repudiates the alibi and charges him with the murder. Then a mystery woman appears with damaging letters against the wife and the young man is freed. We learn, however, that the mystery woman is actually the wife, who has perjured herself because she felt direct testimony for her husband would not have freed him. But when the young man turns his back on his wife for another woman, we realize he really was the murderer. Then Miss Christie gives us a triple-flip ending that leaves the audience gasping, while serving up justice to the young man.

(Royalty, $50-$25.)

THE MOUSETRAP

The longest-run straight play in London history.

Melodrama. 3 acts. By Agatha Christie.

5 men, 3 women. Interior.

The author of *Ten Little Indians* and *Witness for the Prosecution* comes forth with another English hit. About a group of strangers stranded in a boarding house during a snow storm, one of whom is a murderer. The suspects include the newly married couple who run the house, a spinster, an architect, a retired Army major, a strange little man who claims his car overturned in a drift, and a feminine jurist. Into their midst comes a policeman, traveling on skiis. He no sooner arrives than the jurist is killed. To get to the rationale of the murderer's pattern, the policeman probes the background of everyone present, and rattles a lot of skeletons. But in another famous Agatha Christie switch finish, it is the policeman—or rather the man disguised as a policeman—who shoulders the blame. Chalk up another superb intrigue for the foremost mystery writer of her half century. Posters and publicity.

(Royalty, $50-$25.)